BRIAN T. FITCH is Gerald Larkin Professor of French at Trinity College and Associate Chairman of Graduate Studies in the Department of French at the University of Toronto.

Critics, theologians, philosophers, and psychoanalysts have written several thousand books, theses, and articles about Camus' fiction. His first published novel, *L'Etranger*, had a unique impact on a whole generation of readers, and his other fiction, although not as well known, has also been influential. However, Camus' fiction so far has not been judged by contemporary critical methods, and 'inter-textuality,' or the study of the interrelationship between Camus' own texts, has not been examined.

The Narcissistic Text: A Reading of Camus' Fiction is the first book devoted to the whole of Camus' fiction to adopt this approach. Brian Fitch uses the critical tools elaborated in the writings of such French formalists as Barthes, Ricardou, and Todorov and draws upon the hermeneutic theory of literature developed by Gadamer and Ricœur. As a result, the self-generating word-play or linguistic narcissism of 'Jonas' and the textual narcissism of *La Peste* are seen to give way, in *L'Etranger*, to a situation where the hermeneutic circle is itself contained within the circularity of autoreprésentation. As for the narcissism of *La Chute*, it concerns the reader himself, since what the text provides is a model of the hermeneutic process. Fitch thus demonstrates that Camus' fiction occupies a significant place in modern literature.

This volume will be of particular interest to those involved in Camus studies or concerned with contemporary critical methodology and literary theory.

The Narcissistic TEXT

A Reading of Camus' Fiction

Brian T. Fitch

UNIVERSITY OF TORONTO PRESS

Toronto Buffalo London

© University of Toronto Press 1982
Toronto Buffalo London
Reprinted in paperback 2017
ISBN 978-0-8020-2426-8 (cloth)
ISBN 978-1-4875-9857-0 (paper)

Canadian Cataloguing in Publication Data

Fitch, Brian T., 1935–
The narcissistic text
Includes index.
ISBN 978-0-8020-2426-8 (bound). ISBN 978-1-4875-9857-0 (pbk.)
1. Camus, Albert, 1913-1960 – Criticism and
interpretation. I. Title.
PQ2605.A3734Z64   848′.91409   C81-094732-3

This book has been published
with the help of a grant from the
Canadian Federation for the Humanities,
using funds provided by the Social Sciences and
Humanities Research Council of Canada,
and a grant from the Subsidized Publications Fund of the
University of Toronto Press.

Pour Michel J. Minard
sans qui cet ouvrage, comme ses précurseurs,
n'aurait jamais vu le jour

Contents

Acknowledgments

Much of the substance of Chapter 1 formed the second half of a paper given at the symposium on 'Albert Camus' Literary Milieu: Arid Lands' at the Texas Tech University, Lubbock, in January 1975, and entitled 'Camus' Desert Hieroglyphics' (cf. *Proceedings of the Comparative Literature Symposium* ed. Wolodmyr T. Zyla and Wendell M. Aycock VIII [1976] 117-31).

A first version of Chapter 2 was published in French under the title '*La Peste* comme texte qui se désigne: analyse des procédés d'auto-représentation' in *Albert Camus* 8, 'Camus romancier: *La Peste*' (1976) 53-71.

Chapter 3 was first published in French under the title '"Jonas" ou la production d'une étoile' in *Albert Camus* 6, 'Camus nouvelliste: *L'Exil et le royaume*' (1973) 51-65, and given as a public lecture entitled 'L'Approche ricardolienne: "Jonas" de Camus' at Victoria College, University of Toronto, in February 1975.

Certain of the key concepts of Chapters 4 and 5 were first evoked in a plenary session lecture on 'Camus' *La Chute* as a Paradigm of the Hermeneutic Process' given at the 19th Australian Universities Language and Literature Association Congress at the University of Queensland in Brisbane in August 1978, and were subsequently developed in a paper entitled 'Le Paradigme herméneutique chez Camus' given at the Second International Conference: 'Albert Camus 1980' at the University of Florida in Gainesville in February 1980 (cf. *Albert Camus 1980* ed. Raymond Gay-Crosier [Gainesville: University Presses of Florida 1980] 32-44), and in an article entitled 'Narcisse interprète: *La Chute* comme modèle herméneutique' to appear in *Albert Camus* 10, 'Nouvelles Approches.'

I wish to express my sincere thanks to Linda Hutcheon and Janet Paterson for their careful reading of my manuscript and their invaluable suggestions. I have been singularly fortunate over the last few years in having had the opportunity to discuss with them the problems involved in the study of the narcissistic literary form.

BTF

Author's Note

Within quotations, SMALL CAPITALS indicate emphasis by myself and *italics* emphasis by the author of the quotation, except in longer quotations set off by space above and below. In those cases, words in italic small capitals indicate emphasis by myself and words in roman type indicate emphasis by the author of the quotation.

Except where indicated otherwise, references to quotations from Camus' texts refer to the pagination of the following editions, designated by the abbreviations below:

I   Albert Camus, *Théâtre, récits, nouvelles* (Paris: Gallimard, 'Bibliothèque de la Pléiade' 1962; 1963 printing)
II   Albert Camus, *Essais* (Paris: Gallimard, 'Bibliothèque de la Pléiade' 1965; 1967 printing)
MH   Albert Camus, *La Mort heureuse* (Paris: Gallimard, 'Cahiers Albert Camus' 1971)

Note that although, bibliographically and commercially speaking, there has been only one *edition* of the above two 'Pléiade' volumes, the pagination varies from one *printing* to the next. It is, moreover, likely that there exist variations in the actual texts between printings. However, to date, no systematic study of this problem has been undertaken.

Introduction

For some forty years now and since well before his premature death in an automobile accident in 1960, Albert Camus has been considered one of the most significant and influential writers of this century. Eloquent testimony to this fact is furnished by the several thousands of articles and books that have been devoted to the man and his work in countless countries on all five continents and in languages as diverse as Russian, Arabic, and Japanese.[1] That this status as one of the 'classics' of French literature would only be disputed precisely within the boundaries of his native land is doubtless due to ideological considerations above all others. His work has attracted the attention not only of literary critics but also of theologians, psychiatrists, political scientists, and philosophers, to name but a few. He is quoted in both the most erudite and the most popular publications. In short, his fame has spread in a manner unparalleled within the lifetime of any other French writer of this century.

However, the concern of this book is not to give an account of and to account for the impact of Albert Camus on his contemporaries and their times, which would be a sociological enterprise not without interest that will, it is to be hoped, be undertaken one day, but rather to re-examine those texts that comprise Camus' fiction: the three novels, *L'Etranger*, *La Peste*, and *La Chute*, together with certain of the short stories gathered together in *L'Exil et le royaume*.[2]

The three novels have long engaged the interest of critics although to varying degrees, *L'Etranger* having been the most actively and the most continuously debated[3] ever since its publication in 1942 (no less than eight books and monographs[4] have been exclusively given over to it) and *La Peste* having been subjected to the least critical scrutiny.[5] As was no doubt inevitable in the case of a novelist who was also not only a dramatist but a philosopher (if we take this term in its more general sense of thinker and essayist), the fiction was long seen as a reflection of and a vehicle for the main concepts expounded in his philosophical essays *Le Mythe de Sisyphe*[6] and *L'Homme révolté*. Where a less simplistic view of his fiction prevailed, Camus was seen to be a descendant of that venerable lineage of French writers generally categorized as *les moralistes*. The Candide-like[7] characteristics of that twentieth-century morality tale *L'Etranger*, so comparable in this respect to Sartre's short story 'L'Enfance d'un chef,'[8] were recognized as readily as *La Chute*[9] could be seen to be a pretext for a series of maxims that depicted all too well twentieth-century civilization. Rieux's chronicle of the plague clearly belonged in the same company. Small wonder then that, to his dismay and consternation, their author saw himself 'institutionalized,' as it were, as a 'classic' almost before the ink had dried on his manuscripts. It is to his credit that, unlike certain practitioners of the French New Novel who have become permanent fixtures of the North American academic scene, he did nothing to capitalize on this situation, although this did not spare him the severe criticism he suffered at the hands of Sartre and his associates[10] with the publication of *L'Homme révolté* in 1951. But then without the latter, Camus' most enigmatic and most fascinating work, *La Chute*, would never have seen the light of day.

Although the striking originality of the style of Camus' first published novel was recognized from the very first reviews it received,[11] its distinctiveness arising paradoxically from its lack of salient features, its colourless neutrality and bare matter-of-factness, relatively little interest was aroused by the formal qualities of *La Peste* and *La Chute*. Even in the case of *L'Etranger*, such considerations were soon subordinated to the more pressing problem of how to interpret the character of its narrator-protagonist, and indeed the enigma that is Meursault has not ceased to fascinate readers and professional critics alike and to send the latter scurrying for their pens. The marked concern with narrative technique[12] was part and parcel of the same problem. An analogous if lesser concern was shown by the critics with the narrative structure of *La Chute*, which for all its theatrical overtones revealed a highly original blending of the monologue and the dialogue. But the interpretation of the character of the judge-penitent proved no less problematic given the difficulty of reconciling his grating cynicism with the publicly applauded humanism of his creator as exemplified in *La Peste* and *L'Homme révolté*. Autobiographical resonances were soon detected and gave rise to an almost exclusive preoccupation with the very particular relationship it appeared to bear to the bitter quarrel between Camus and Sartre.[13] As for *La Peste*, it was read solely on the level of its story as both an allegory of the German occupation of France and a rather obvious vehicle for the Camusian version of André Malraux's message of virile human fraternity, a kind of latter-day rewrite of *La Condition humaine*.

The evolution of Camus' fiction was seen above all in terms of thematics. The proponent of the Absurd (*L'Etranger*) gave way to the proponent of Revolt (*La Peste*) who, in turn, was succeeded by the proponent of Duplicity (*La Chute*). Or, in slightly different terms, one passed from the innocent carefreeness of the noble savage to the moral concern of the committed humanist and hence to the moral anguish of the guilt-ridden introspective. Throughout all three novels ran the insistent theme of judges and judgment: parodied and condemned in *L'Etranger*, sympathized with in *La Peste*, and finally depicted from within in the person of Clamence.

Thematics on the level of the writer's total fictive output, the character of the (anti-)heroes of *L'Etranger* and *La Chute*, the all-too-exemplary tales of *L'Etranger* and *La Peste* – these were the object of critical scrutiny. If it proved difficult to conceive of a single Camusian fictive universe to which all his characters belonged, in the manner of the Balzacian, Bernanosian, or even the Malrucian universes, each of the novels nonetheless conjured up a world of its own even if the world in question was heavily dependent for its particular climate on the character of its narrator and, more particularly, on the tone of voice of his narration.[14] If this corpus of fiction could not begin to compete with the great novelistic creations of a Balzac or a Zola in their depiction of the multiple strata of contemporary society through the evocation of a galaxy of motley characters, it nonetheless introduced us to characters as complex and intriguing as any reader could wish for, few in number yet as distinctive and particular as any real-life acquaintance. In short, Camus was, in the final analysis, a traditional novelist, classical in that very same understatement he had analysed in his essay on Madame de la Fayette ('L'Intelligence et l'échafaud,' I, 1187-94), even if his preferred novelistic form was that of the traditional French *récit* of a Benjamin Constant or an André Gide, certainly closer to the latter, moreover, than to his contemporary Jean-Paul Sartre.

However, something more remained to be said about Camus' art as a novelist. The very particular tone of voice of each of the three narrators, referred to above, and the distinctive climate it suggested could easily alert the reader to the marked degree of stylization[15] in the texts that was responsible for these effects, a stylization Camus had also attributed to the classical French novel of the seventeenth century.[16] The world of the fiction was perceived by the reader as through a glass darkly, a glass that, in the case of *L'Etranger*, Sartre had likened to the glass door of a telephone booth.[17] The reader's vision of that world was somehow blurred, his angle of vision oblique. The language of the text, through its high degree of stylization, was no longer transparent, an unequivocal pointer towards the fictive reality beyond. It had taken on a certain opacity, the opacity of its own material existence as language. With this relative opacification of the language of the text, language drew attention to itself and away from the fiction that provided its ostensible raison d'être. It revealed a preoccupation with self, a certain narcissism.

It is precisely this self-consciousness of the Camusian text that this book explores. Formal narcissism of this kind, together with the process of autorepresentation that is at the same time its symptom and its vehicle, has come to the fore in the intense debate that has been taking place in France over the last twenty years or so around literary theory. It is indeed one of the essential features of our present-day conception of the literary text and its functioning. Hence, one of the main objectives of the following pages is to reveal these fictive texts of Camus as being of more than passing interest to the contemporary literary theoretician and critic and as properly belonging to what the French call *la modernité* in spite of their reputation as traditional works in which, to use Jean Ricardou's distinction, *l'euphorie du récit* clearly prevails over any incipient *contestation du récit*.[18]

It would, however, be difficult to conceive of any adequate account of Camus' novels that did not recognize the particular rôle of the reader.[19] The experience of the reader of Camus' fiction is by no means a comfortable, reassuring one: the demands made upon him by these texts are insistent and ever-changing, disconcerting and unsettling, to the point that I have claimed elsewhere that it is the reader who is the true occupant of Clamence's *malconfort*.[20] This is, incidentally, one of the main justifications for considering Camus as a precursor of the French new novelists. One could well maintain that his art as a novelist lies as much in the skilful and continual manipulation of his reader as in the numerous and subtle variations he effects in the narrative perspective of his works. It should therefore come as no surprise to learn that the reading process and the activity of interpretation that it necessarily gives rise to are themselves taken up within the mechanism of autorepresentation in the case of *L'Etranger* and *La Chute*. In the former text, the hermeneutic circle is itself encompassed within the circular process of the text's reflection upon itself. In the latter, the reader is, or becomes, in a very real sense one of the protagonists of a work that is an enactment of the hermeneutic experience. It is for this reason that my analysis of the texts draws not only on the writings of the French formalists such as Jean Ricardou, Tzvetan Todorov, and Roland Barthes but also on the theories of the present-day practitioners of the hermeneutic tradition, notably Hans-Georg Gadamer and Paul Ricœur. This book thus represents a coming together of formalism and hermeneutics necessitated by the specific characteristics of Camus' fiction.

The Narcissistic Text

The Writing on the Blackboard

One finds in Camus' fiction a curious and unremarked predilection for blackboards and analogous objects that fulfil the same function as circumscribed surfaces to be written upon. There is the blackboard on which the rebel Arabs leave Daru's death sentence at the end of the short story 'L'Hôte.' The long process during which Joseph Grand labours painstakingly over the single sentence he seeks to perfect is also worked out on a blackboard, his room being described thus: 'On remarquait seulement un rayon de bois blanc garni de deux ou trois dictionnaires, et un tableau noir sur lequel on pouvait lire encore, à demi effacés, les mots "allées fleuries".' (I, 1240) A little later in *La Peste*, the same blackboard reappears serving a different function: 'Il écrivait donc des mots latins sur son tableau. Il recopiait à la craie bleue la partie des mots qui changeait suivant les déclinaisons et les conjugaisons, et, à la craie rouge, celle qui ne changeait pas.' (I, 1241) But this is not the only blackboard to figure in this novel, for the presence of another one is remarked upon in the evocation of the former class-room that has been converted to serve as a hospital: 'il fit assez jour, enfin, pour qu'au fond de la salle, sur le tableau noir demeuré en place, on pût distinguer les traces d'anciennes formules d'équation ...' (I, 1391) Even the door to Cottard's apartment takes on the function of this traditional class-room accessory: 'sur la porte de gauche, Rieux lut, tracé à la craie: "Entrez, je suis pendu."' (I, 1229) More curiously, at the end of another of the short stories, 'Jonas ou l'artiste au travail,' we find the artist's canvas being put to the same purpose, one word taking the place of the painting it was intended for: 'Rateau regardait la toile, entièrement blanche, au centre de laquelle Jonas avait seulement écrit, en très petits caractères, un mot qu'on pouvait déchiffrer, mais dont on ne savait s'il fallait y lire *solitaire* ou *solidaire*.' (I, 1652)

Blackboards have a definite affinity with both the printed page and the sheets of the writer's manuscript: they have an analogous rectangular shape and are intended to bear the traces of the written language. Moreover, contrary to the actual blackboards referred to above, Jonas's canvas also has in common with the sheet of paper its whiteness. It is significant that none of this family of objects remains blank in these texts. Each bears an inscription, more or less clear and decipherable according to the circumstances of the fiction. One is tempted to see in this phenomenon a reflection of the very page of the text that forms part of the book in which it figures. Both Daru's and Grand's blackboards are exemplary in this respect. (I shall leave aside Jonas's canvas for a later chapter since it has added implications.)

Daru's blackboard is evoked, interestingly enough, both (and only) at the beginning and the end of 'L'Hôte.' Immediately following the first introductory paragraph of the short story, we come upon this evocation: 'Il [Daru] traversa la salle de classe vide et glacée. Sur le tableau noir les quatre fleuves de France, dessinés avec quatre craies de couleurs différentes, coulaient vers leur estuaire depuis trois jours.' (I, 1609) It is not until the very last paragraph of the text that actual writing appears on the blackboard: 'Derrière lui, sur le tableau noir, entre les méandres de fleuves français s'étalait, tracée à la craie par une main malhabile, l'inscription qu'il venait de lire: "Tu as livré notre frère. Tu paieras."' (I, 1621) It is as though the sole function of the intervening twelve pages of text were to produce the writing on the blackboard. In other words, the substance of the short story, the tale of Daru's treatment of the Arab prisoner, can be viewed as a mere pretext in the two senses of the word: a pretext for the production of a text that is none other than the writing on the blackboard and a pre-text in the sense that it necessarily precedes that two-sentence text. However, the very process of producing the words on the blackboard results in the production of the actual text of the story 'L'Hôte.' Moreover, by the same token, the shorter text is also a condensed representation of the latter, which it reproduces in miniature. The relationship of the two sentences on the blackboard to the text of the short story on the printed page is precisely that of the microcosm to the macrocosm. It is for such a relationship, that of a microcosm reflecting and reproducing a macrocosm, that Claude-Edmonde Magny[1] coined the literary neologism *mise-en-abyme*.

An analogous situation can be seen to pertain in the case of Joseph Grand's famous sentence laboriously worked out and revised on his own blackboard in *La Peste*. However, there is an important difference, since Grand's sentence figures not once but on a number of occasions in the text of the novel as we follow its gradual evolution whereby the initial words 'allées fleuries' (I, 1240) become a sentence: 'Par une belle matinée du mois de mai, une élégante amazone parcourait, sur une superbe jument alezane, les allées fleuries du Bois de Boulogne.' (I, 1302) This is then modified to form: 'Par une belle matinée de mai, une svelte amazone, montée sur une superbe jument, parcourait les allées fleuries du Bois de Boulogne.' (I, 1327) Which then becomes: 'Par une belle matinée de mai, une svelte amazone montée sur une somptueuse jument alezane parcourait les allées pleines de fleurs du Bois de Boulogne.' (I, 1328) To be finalized in the following form: 'Par une belle matinée de mai, une svelte amazone, montée sur une somptueuse jument alezane, parcourait, au milieu des fleurs, les allées du Bois ...' (I, 1432) While not wishing to go as far as one critic who saw in the evolution of this one sentence nothing less than 'a kind of history in miniature of the evolution of contemporary Occidental mentality',[2] it is, I believe, clear that this is not the static reflection in miniature of the finalized and immutable text of the whole novel but rather the *mise-en-abyme* of the productive process itself through which the novel came into being, what Lucien Dällenbach has termed the 'mise-en-abyme de l'énonciation,'[3] *énonciation*[4] comprising both the production and the reception of the text. It is a mirror reflection of its actual generation, a process described in detail in Chapter 3, devoted to 'Jonas.' It is hardly surprising that this should be the function of the blackbord image since, contrary to what was said earlier about the representation of both the manuscript page and its printed counterpart, the blackboard, due to the possibility it offers not only of inscription but also of endless correction and modification of what has already been written upon it, is clearly a more fitting mirror image of the former than the latter.

I shall be returning to the various evocations of Grand's sentence in a slightly different context in Chapter 2, on *La Peste*. Suffice it to remark here that the difficulty that Grand experiences in the working out of his sentence, the laborious nature of his months-long enterprise, if it brings to mind by its apparent futility the grotesque figure of the old man in the same novel who spends his time spitting on the cats and transferring peas from one receptacle to another, is also not so dissimilar from the painstaking, meticulous manner in which Rieux relates the events that make up his chronicle. The various transcriptions of the stages in the evolution of Grand's sentence hence function, on the first level, as an *intra*-textual mirror whereby the fiction reflects the narratives to which it more immediately owes its existence. It is only subsequently that their activity shifts onto the other level encompassing the actual production of the text, its actual origins in the process of writing.

If blackboards are not uncommon in Camus' fiction, images of writing, of linguistic signs, are even less so. It is often the sky that takes the place of the blackboard studied earlier. Indeed, whereas the blackboard constituted a kind of photographic negative of the white sheet of paper, the sky restitutes the positive since it, too, is characterized in these southern climes by the same blinding whiteness. Thus, in the short story 'Le Renégat ou un esprit confus,' the sky is described as a 'plaque de tôle chauffée à blanc.' (I, 1582) It is hardly surprising that just as the linguistic signs stand out from the white sheet of paper they are written or printed on, it is precisely against the backcloth formed by the North African sky, 'blanc de chaleur' (II, 58) in the essay 'Noces,' that certain signs are to be read: 'Car cette ville squelette, vue de si haut dans le soir finissant et dans les vols blancs des pigeons autour de l'arc de triomphe, n'inscrivait pas sur le ciel les signes de la conquête et de l'ambition.' (II, 65) While the 'signes' in question are not here designated explicitly as being linguistic in nature, the metaphor used to describe the relationship that man establishes with the desert is, curiously, manifestly linguistic: 'Par elle (ma peau), auparavant, je DECHIFFRAIS L'ECRITURE du monde. Il y traçait les signes de sa tendresse ou de sa colère ... Mais si longuement frotté du vent ... je perdais conscience du dessin que traçait mon corps.' (II, 62) The uniformity and visual monotony of the desert, together with the blinding and unceasing sunlight that pervades it and from which there is no escape, make of its landscape an ideal backcloth that shares these attributes with the white sheet of paper awaiting the writer's pen or the printer's ink. Nowhere does the

Camusian text refer to itself so clearly and offer a more explicit trans-
cription of its own origins in the act of writing than in this detail of the
desert landscape noted by Janine in 'La Femme adultère': 'Tout
autour, un troupeau de dromadaires immobiles, minuscules à cette
distance, formaient sur le sol gris les signes d'une étrange écriture
dont il fallait déchiffrer le sens.' (I, 1567) Even with the coming of
night (and the consequent setting of the sun), when the act of writing
necessarily gives way to the inner unfurling of mental imagery in the
form of a fresco of curiously shaped animals, the same desert back-
ground appears: 'La nuit commença. Des images venaient. De
grands animaux fantastiques qui hochaient la tête au-dessus de
paysages désertiques.' (MH, 199) Something of the same effect as in
this passage from *La Mort heureuse*, Camus' posthumously published
novel, is created by another fresco with the interplay and contrast
between a white background and the dark human forms set off
against it. It is the scene presented by the harbour of the Kasbah in
Algiers, as depicted in the essay 'L'Eté à Alger': 'Le port est
dominé par le jeu de cubes blancs de la Kasbah. Quand on est au
niveau de l'eau, sur le fond blanc cru de la ville arabe, les corps
déroulent une frise cuivrée. Et, à mesure qu'on avance dans le
mois d'août et que le soleil grandit, le blanc des maisons se fait plus
aveuglant et les peaux prennent une chaleur plus sombre.' (II, 69)

One of the most striking evocations of the desert figures in the
remarkable and, in many ways, puzzling short story 'Le Renégat.'
The following description, which recalls the linguistic signs formed by
the dromedaries as seen by Janine, will serve as a useful transition to a
detailed consideration of this short story that will bring out its special
significance in the present context: 'les chameaux fuient droit vers
l'horizon, où un geyser d'oiseaux noirs vient de s'élever dans le ciel
inaltéré.' (I, 1590)

One of the many peculiarities of 'Le Renégat' is that, with the
murder scene and the scene in the mortuary in *L'Etranger*, it contains
one of the very few hallucinatory passages in all of Camus' works.
This hallucinatory quality can obviously be attributed, on the level of
the fictive universe, quite literally to the mind of the protagonist who
is, as in the case of Meursault before him, hallucinating. However, on
the formal level of the writing, these passages have a distinctly visual
quality, rare in Camus, that makes an indelible impression on the

reader's mind. These evocations curiously happen to be characterized by the same blinding whiteness, whether it be in the earlier novel or in the description, in the short story, of 'la ville de sel, au creux de cette cuvette pleine de chaleur.' (I, 1581) This is very clear from the following passage:

Sur chacun des murs droits, taillés à coups de pic, grossièrement rabotés, les entailles laissées par le pic se hérissent en écailles éblouissantes, du sable blond épars les jaunit un peu, sauf quand le vent nettoie les murs droits et les terrasses, tout resplendit alors dans une blancheur fulgurante, sous le ciel nettoyé lui aussi jusqu'à son écorce bleue. Je devenais aveugle, dans ces jours où l'immobile incendie crépitait pendant des heures sur la surface des terrasses blanches qui semblaient se rejoindre toutes comme si, un jour d'autrefois, ils avaient attaqué ensemble une montagne de sel, l'avaient d'abord aplanie, puis, à même la masse, avaient creusé les rues, l'intérieur des maisons, et les fenêtres, ou comme si, oui, c'est mieux, ils avaient découpé leur enfer blanc et brûlant avec un chalumeau d'eau bouillante ... dans ce creux au milieu du désert ... (I, 1581)

Although there is nothing in these particular lines to attenuate the all-pervasive dazzling whiteness created by the light-reflecting salt, nothing black or merely darker in colour to suggest characters on a page, one is struck by the impression of relief and clear-cut texture with the walls 'taillés à coup de pic,' the 'écailles eblouissantes' left by the pick and appearing to stand out sharply, and the hollowed-out streets, houses, and windows, all creating the effect of the mountain's having been cut away by 'un chalumeau d'eau bouillante ... dans ce creux au milieu du désert.' Here it is as though the characters had not been traced in ink but rather embossed in the very whiteness of the paper. Moreover, the physical effort that has obviously had to be exerted in the process of hollowing out the salt, 'taill[é] à coup de pic,' bears eloquent, if figurative, testimony to the mental exertion entailed in the forging of language by the writer in the act of literary creation.

In fact, as Linda Hutcheon has very convincingly demonstrated in her remarkable essay '"Le Renégat ou un esprit confus" comme Nouveau Récit,'[5] the whole of this text can be read as an allegory of the act of writing. The 'chalumeau' or pipe is not the only trace of the writing instrument in the text, for the evocation of the fetish's head suggests the pen's metallic nib: 'j'ai vu le fétiche, sa double tête de hâche, son nez de fer tordu comme un serpent.' (I, 1584) Yet another image evoking written characters on a page emerges here: 'ils passent, silencieux, couverts de leurs voiles de deuil, dans la blancheur minérale des rues ...' (I, 1582) Where does this strange town of the savages lie? Precisely at the meeting place between the black characters and the white page, 'à la frontière de la terre des noirs et du pays blanc, où s'élève la ville de sel.' (I, 1580)

The dialectic of black and white reappears constantly in the descriptions right down to the footwear of its inhabitants 'dans les sandales rouges et noires, leurs pieds brillants de sel.' (I, 1582) The richness of the allegory emerges from these remarkable passages where there is nothing schematic or abstract, and hence intellectualized, that would immediately suggest allegoric intent and detract from the evocative power of the language. On the contrary, the visual impact of these scenes with their strange, barely human forms flitting silently across an otherworldly landscape and their stark interplay of blackness and whiteness gives them a nightmarish quality that continues to grip the reader's imagination long after he has laid down the book. It is as though they had been summoned up from out of the darkest recesses of the human mind. However, my intention here is not to suggest that the source of the imagery lies in the subconscious – whatever the merits or otherwise of such a hypothesis – but rather to claim that nowhere else is Camus' writing evocatively more powerful, visually more effective:

le froid de la nuit les fige un à un dans leurs coquillages de gemme, habitants nocturnes d'une banquise sèche, esquimaux noirs grelottant tout d'un coup dans leurs igloos cubiques. Noirs, oui, car ils sont habillés de longues étoffes noires et le sel qui envahit jusqu'aux ongles, qu'on remâche amèrement dans le sommeil polaire des nuits, le sel qu'on boit dans l'eau qui vient à l'unique source au creux d'une entaille brillante, laisse parfois sur leurs robes sombres des traces semblables aux traînées des escargots après la pluie. (I, 1581)

To quote Linda Hutcheon, 'nous avons ici le négatif photographique des traces (les traînées) de l'encre (la pluie) noire (le sel) sur une page blanche (étoffes noires)'[6] – although this negative had been preceded by its positive equivalent with the image of the 'esquimaux noirs grelottant tout d'un coup dans leurs igloos cubiques,' where the *shivering* silhouettes of the Eskimos suggest the squiggles from the writer's pen.

More interesting still in the present context is the expression 'le sommeil polaire des nuits,' which echoes the 'nuit polaire' evoked in *Le Mythe de Sisyphe*, that characterizes lucid despair, that 'veille de l'esprit d'où se lèvera peut-être cette clarté blanche et intacte qui dessine chaque objet dans la lumière de l'intelligence' (II, 146), and where black and white come together as a succinct visual paradox that can be seen to symbolize paper and ink. For although it is a question, in the essay, of pictorial images rather than linguistic signs, the 'clarté blanche et intacte' could well evoke the virgin whiteness of the writer's sheet of paper. The same contradictory coming-together of black and white is found in the depiction of the desert landscape in the essay 'Eté,' where the landscape is described as 'noire de soleil' (II, 55) and the light that prevails is seen to be 'si éclatante qu'elle en devient noire et blanche.' (II, 847) The following evocation of the effect created by the sunlight points up the same phenomenon, that is far from going generally unremarked:

sa lumière (du soleil), à force d'épaisseur, coagule l'univers et ses formes dans un EBLOUISSEMENT OBSCUR. Mais cela peut se dire autrement et je voudrais, devant cette CLARTE BLANCHE ET NOIRE qui, pour moi, a toujours été celle de la vérité, m'expliquer simplement sur cette absurdité que je connais trop pour supporter qu'on en disserte sans nuances. Parler d'elle, au demeurant, nous mènera de nouveau au soleil. (II, 861)

We shall have occasion in the next chapter on *La Peste* to appreciate not only how the characters on the page indulge in the kind of self-reflective process described and thereby suggest the very activity of the writer that underlies and would appear chronologically to precede their existence as text (although, in fact, as we shall see later, this activity is contemporaneous with the unfolding of the text within which it is inscribed for all eternity), but also how the tangible, material object without which they would not be perceptible – the paper which provides their material habitat – is also *re*presented within the text.

However, to conclude the present chapter, I should like to return to the point made in my introduction concerning stylization, which I can here illustrate in detail and which will serve as a useful transition to the chapters that follow.

The way that the text throws up an image of the writing process itself and draws attention to the materiality of language which is, of course, part and parcel of the writer's experience is but a further development of the text's self-conscious turning away from the fiction it normally serves to bring to existence in the mind's eye of the reader. The text turns in on itself, thus generating a series of mirror reflections of its own activity and exists for its own sake as it unfolds in a weaving-out process whereby text takes on tangible texture through the continual interplay of signifier with signifier as well as between signifier and signified (the third relation between signified and signified being primarily responsible for the constitution of the fictive universe itself). The more readily recognized tendency of the language from which it is woven to be lost sight of because of that transparent quality that enables the non-linguistic world to rise up in an unobstructed vision and realize what Jean Ricardou has named the 'referential illusion'[7] has receded into the background as language has taken back to itself and reclaimed the material opacity that it shares with other objects.

The comparison that Ortega y Gasset has made in *The Dehumanization of Art* could not be more appropriate here. He likens the relationship that exists between language and the fictive universe to that pertaining between the windowpane and the garden that lies beyond it:

Looking at the garden we adjust our eyes in such a way that the ray of vision travels through the pane without delay and rests on the shrubs and flowers. Since we are focusing on the garden and our ray of vision is directed toward it, we do not see the window but look clear through it. The purer the glass, the less we see it. But we can also deliberately disregard the garden and, withdrawing the ray of vision, detain it at the window. We then lose sight of the garden; what we still behold of it is a confused mass of color which appears pasted to the pane. Hence to see the garden and to see the windowpane are two incompatible operations which exclude one another because they require different adjustments.[8]

Camus' novels are conceived in such a manner that the reader is never allowed to lose sight of the existence of the glass, which relentlessly imposes itself upon his attention. It is because of the glass's coming so obtrusively and persistently between him and the world of its characters, subordinating as it were the activity of his mind's eye to that of his real eye, the sensorial organ that picks out the configuration of the letters and words on the page before him, that he finds his naïve expectations as a traditional novel-reader (and a traditional-novel reader), in the final analysis, frustrated,[9] as readers of *L'Etranger* and *La Chute* have found time and again:

But not many people are capable of adjusting their perceptive apparatus to the pane and the transparency that is the work of art. Instead they look right through it and revel in the human reality with which the work deals. When they are invited to let go of this prey and to direct their attention to the work of art itself they will say that they cannot see such a thing, which indeed they cannot, because it is all artistic transparency and without substance.[10]

Curiously we find an explicit illustration of Ortega y Gasset's analysis in Camus' posthumously published novel-text *La Mort heureuse*, which merely confirms explicitly what remains implicit in his later texts. It reveals that, all appearances to the contrary, there is no possibility of the text's losing sight of itself, so to speak, of its losing its own self-consciousness. The tissue of language never effaces itself entirely in favour of the fiction it points towards. Joseph Grand's ambition will never be realized: 'Quand je serai arrivé à rendre parfaitement le tableau que j'ai dans l'imagination ... alors le reste sera plus facile et surtout l'illusion sera telle, dès le début, qu'il sera possible de dire: "Chapeau bas"!' (I, 1302) The illusion is never complete and definitive. Nowhere is its instability more vividly allegorized than in the scene, from *La Mort heureuse*, where Mersault is looking out through a windowpane bearing condensation and where it is perhaps not entirely fanciful to see in the image of the big blackbirds those same linguistic signs whose material presence yields to the world of fiction:

A perte de vue et à distances régulières, de grands oiseaux noirs ... tournaient en rond dans un vol lent et lourd, et parfois l'un d'eux quittait le groupe, rasait la terre, presque confondu avec elle, et s'éloignait d'un même vol gras, inter-minablement jusqu'à ce qu'il fût assez loin pour se détacher comme un point noir dans le ciel commençant. Mersault avait effacé de ses mains la buée de la vitre et il regardait avidement par les longues raies que ses doigts avaient laissées sur le verre. De la terre désolée au ciel sans couleur se levait pour lui l'image d'un monde ingrat où pour la première fois, il revenait enfin à lui-même ... Mersault écrasa ses larmes et ses lèvres contre le verre froid. De nouveau la vitre se troubla, la plaine disparut. (MH, 116-17)

2

The Autoreferential Text:
La Peste

La Peste is a text which often speaks of other texts. These other texts are, moreover, of all kinds, ranging from the very short to the very long and their status varies between the aesthetic and the practical. It could even be claimed that the real subject of *La Peste* is none other than the text in all its various forms.

This work starts out by explicitly designating itself as a text: 'Les curieux événements qui font le sujet de cette CHRONIQUE se sont produits en 194., à Oran.' (I, 1217) Texts or parts or aspects of texts are mentioned some 170 times[1] within *La Peste* and one finds fifty or so different terms that fulfil this function. For the purposes of this chapter, the numerous forms of writing referred to can be classified in several categories. In addition to the 'chronique' itself, several other literary genres are evoked such as the 'roman,' 'roman policier,' 'épopée,' 'récit,' and 'carnets,' as well as the more general terms 'histoire' and 'texte.' Non-literary forms of writing are also mentioned, whether it be the 'feuilleton,' the 'lettre,' the 'traité,' the 'travail (écrit),' the 'note,' the 'bulletin,' the 'journal' or the 'télégramme.' Other terms belong to the realm of journalism and government bureaucracy, such as 'reportage,' 'communiqué,' 'décrets,' 'dépêche,' 'déclaration préfectorale,' 'déclaration administrative,' 'annonce,' 'déposition,' 'publication de statistiques,' 'arrêt,' 'arrêté,' and 'rapport.' There are also those mini-texts that serve, for example, to provide various forms of information: 'curriculum vitae,' 'bulletin de renseignements,' 'ordonnance,' 'inscription,' 'écriteau,' 'affiche,' 'pancarte,' 'mot d'ordre,' 'laisser-passer,' and 'message.' An analogous function is fulfilled by 'l'indicateur Chaix,' 'le graphique,' 'une radiographie,' 'tableau de surveillance,' and 'feuilles de statistiques.' Further terms designate the material character of the written text as in the case of 'livre,' 'ouvrage,' 'documents,' 'fiche,' 'dossiers,' 'livre de chevet,' 'papiers,' 'manuscrit,' 'feuille,' 'feuille manuscrite,' and 'pages.' Finally, there are other constitutive parts of the text: 'mots,' 'mots justes,' 'signes,' 'formules,' 'phrases,' 'bouts de phrase,' 'cliché,' 'clause de style,' 'longue période,' 'lignes,' 'observations,' and 'remarques.' This summary enumeration will suffice to illustrate the considerable variety of terms that evoke the written language in its different forms. And this is not the least remarkable aspect of the vocabulary of *La Peste*.

To speak of texts, to evoke the text in its various possible guises, is, when what is speaking is itself a text, necessarily to speak of oneself. In other words, I have just enumerated diverse fashions in which the text goes about referring to itself. But to speak of oneself is not the only way to refer to oneself. The autorepresentation the text indulges in consists of a whole range of procedures to which *La Peste* bears eloquent witness.

Few readers of this novel could remain unaware of the important rôle played by language and the inadequacies of language in its thematic texture. The attention paid by the representatives of authority to the precise wording of official statements and their correlation to the laws of the land is a clear source of satirical effect in Camus' depiction of how Oran's administration is reluctant to come to grips with the first tell-tale signs of the outbreak of the plague. This is contrasted with Rieux's matter-of-fact no-nonsense practicality that insists on calling a spade a spade: 'il fallait des mesures complètes, non des phrases ...' (I, 1265), he points out, and 'Ce n'est pas une question de vocabulaire, c'est une question de temps.' (I, 1256) What is important is not the words used to describe what is happening but the practical measures that are to be put into effect. In other words, language can have no real grasp on the concrete reality of human suffering:

Les médecins se consultèrent et Richard finit par dire:
— Il faut donc que nous prenions la responsabilité d'agir comme si la maladie était la peste.
*   La formule fut chaleureusement approuvée:*

– C'est ainsi votre avis, mon cher confrère? demanda Richard.
– La formule m'est indifférente, dit Rieux. (I, 1256-7)

– no more than the numerical language of statistics can provide a meaningful account of the death toll of pestilence, as Rieux discovers in attempting to appreciate the dimensions of the situation:

Il essayait de rassembler dans son esprit ce qu'il savait de cette maladie. Des chiffres flottaient dans sa mémoire et il se disait que la trentaine de grandes pestes que l'histoire a connues avait fait près de cent millions de morts. Mais qu'est-ce que cent millions de morts? Quand on a fait la guerre, c'est à peine si on sait déjà ce qu'est un mort. Et puisqu'un homme mort n'a de poids que si on l'a vu mort, cent millions de cadavres semés à travers l'histoire ne sont qu'une fumée dans l'imagination. (I, 1246)

Language and statistics are but two facets of the phenomenon of abstraction[2] that is one of the main adversaries in the struggle against the plague.

However, the interplay of major themes within the work is not part of my present concern. What is more pertinent is the way in which language has a tendency to provide a commentary upon itself, so that we read that 'les mots "transiger," "faveur," "exception" n'avaient plus de sens' (I, 1272) and that 'le mot même de "nouveauté" avait perdu son sens.' (I, 1397) Language thereby draws attention, to itself, no longer giving way to what is here the fictive reality it ostensibly designates. This is true not only on the level of the evocation of the drama that is played out before the reader but also on that of the other dimension of the fiction which is constituted by the actual telling of the tale. The narrative is characterized, before all else, by certain 'précautions de langage' (I, 1220) which manifest themselves time and time again in the discourse of our chronicler:

Le docteur remarqua que Grand, parlant de Cottard, l'appelait toujours 'le désespéré.' Il employa même à un moment l'expression 'résolution fatale.' Ils discutèrent sur le motif du suicide et Grand se montra tatillon sur le choix des termes. On s'arrêta enfin sur les mots 'chagrins intimes.' Le commissaire demanda si rien dans l'attitude de Cottard ne laissait prévoir ce qu'il appelait 'sa détermination.' (I, 1241)

Not the least curious aspect of *La Peste* is the paradox that, while the text insists that what really matters, the experience of the plague, 'n'est pas une affaire de vocabulaire' (I, 1256), its own status does tend to become reduced to a mere question of words and language. The reason is not only that the theme of the inadequacy of language ends up, through a process of almost inevitable contamination, by undermining its own linguistic vehicle, but also that the neutrality and objectivity the narrator cultivates gives rise to a kind of very distinctive, obtrusive verbosity which obviously has nothing to do with the wordiness of gossip or affectation that arises from a quite different motivation. The language of the narrative manages to be obtrusive precisely because it seems to be trying too hard to be discreet and with this end in view, uses so many circumlocutions and reformulations, taking, so to speak, two steps backward for every step with which it carries the narrative forward. It goes without saying that in drawing attention to itself, the language of the novel, by the same token, necessarily draws attention to its own material medium: the text.

Let us now turn to the actual devices at work in the process of autorepresentation. I shall first of all trace and map out a series of reflections operating within the confines of the text whereby the latter appears to pause to reflect upon itself before moving forward, picking up again what has already been evoked and repeating it, and hence *re*presenting itself. Thus the progression of the text matches that of the narrator's discourse. The following passage once again raises the problem of the inadequacy of language, this time in the form of telegrams and letters:

Même la légère satisfaction d'écrire nous fut refusée ... Les télégrammes restèrent alors notre seule ressource. Des êtres que liaient l'intelligence, le cœur et la chair, en furent réduits à chercher les signes de cette communion ancienne dans les majuscules d'une dépêche de dix mots. Et comme, en fait, les formules qu'on peut utiliser dans un télégramme sont vite épuisées, de longues vies communes ou des passions douloureuses se résumèrent rapidement dans un échange périodique de formules toutes faites comme: 'Vais bien. Pense à toi. Tendresse.'

Certains d'entre nous, cependant, s'obstinaient à écrire et imaginaient sans trêve, pour correspondre avec l'extérieur, des combinaisons qui finissaient toujours par se révéler illusoires. Quand même quelques-uns des moyens que nous avions imaginés réussissaient, nous n'en savions rien, ne recevant pas de réponse. Pendant des semaines, nous fûmes réduits alors à recommencer sans cesse la même lettre, à recopier les mêmes appels, si bien qu'au bout d'un certain temps, les mots qui d'abord étaient sortis tout saignants de notre cœur se vidaient de leur sens. Nous les recopiions alors machinalement, essayant de donner au moyen de ces phrases mortes des signes de notre vie difficile. (I, 1272-3)

The first sentence of the second paragraph represents a veritable allegory of the act of writing: the writer's fate is none other than that of imagining 'des combinaisons qui fini[ssent] toujours par s'avérer illusoires' inasmuch as language, in the final analysis, refers to nothing but itself. But my main concern here is with the image of being reduced 'à recommencer sans cesse la même lettre,' for it produces its mirror image in the shape of the character of Joseph Grand, who devotes his whole existence to rewriting the same sentence which, 'indéfiniment recopiée, remaniée, enrichie ou appauvrie' (I 1432), constitutes the sum total of the manuscript that the municipal employee shows to Rieux.

Grand is first of all introduced to the reader as somebody who 'ne trouvait pas ses mots' (I, 1252), a problem which 'l'empêchait toujours d'écrire la lettre de réclamation qu'il méditait':

A l'en croire, il se sentait particulièrement empêché d'employer le mot 'droit' sur lequel il n'était pas ferme, ni celui de 'promesses' qui aurait impliqué qu'il réclamait son dû et aurait par conséquent revêtu un caractère de hardiesse, peu compatible avec la modestie des fonctions qu'il occupait. D'un autre côté, il se refusait à utiliser les termes de 'bienveillance,' 'solliciter,' 'gratitude,' dont il estimait qu'ils ne se conciliaient pas avec sa dignité personnelle. C'est ainsi que faute de trouver le mot juste, notre concitoyen continua d'exercer ses obscures fonctions jusqu'à un âge assez avancé. (I, 1252)

Quite apart from the recurrence here of the stress on language and the difficulty of bringing the latter into line, or even contact, with the reality (psychological, in this case) to which one seeks to give expression ('pour évoquer des émotions si simples, cependant, le moindre mot lui coûtait mille peines,' we are told.) '"Ah! Docteur, disait-il, je voudrais bien apprendre à m'exprimer".' [I, 1253]), what should be noted is that the paragraph in question is, as it were, framed by the same observation. Just as the previous paragraph ended with the words: 'Enfin, et surtout, Joseph Grand ne trouvait pas ses mots' (I, 1252), the present one ends thus: 'Il continuait de chercher ses mots.' (I, 1252) Now, these two sentences point to another level of the text which is not that of the fiction as such (as was the case with the evocation of the character Grand), but that of the narration. They apply not only to Grand himself but also to Rieux in his function as narrator. Curiously the sentence with which the very next paragraph begins itself illustrates the point I am making: 'Dans un certain sens, on peut bien dire que sa vie était exemplaire.' (I, 1252) The narrator too appears to be constantly searching for words: 'Ce qui est plus original dans notre ville est la difficulté qu'on peut y trouver à mourir. Difficulté, d'ailleurs, n'est pas le bon mot et il serait plus juste de parler d'inconfort' (I, 1218) – an 'inconfort,' one might add, that is far removed from the 'malconfort' of the inveterately voluble narrator of *La Chute*! Although the 'précautions de langage' (I, 1220) which he continually has recourse to can appear to represent a striving after 'le mot juste' (I, 1252), the latter nevertheless repeatedly eludes him and any impression of linguistic precision and accuracy soon gives way to a string of formulations that are all equally approximative, much in the manner, as we have already seen, that all the talk by the text about the irrelevance of language itself takes on the appearance of just so much talk or verbiage:

On dira SANS DOUTE que cela n'est pas particulier à notre ville et qu'EN SOMME tous nos contemporains sont ainsi. SANS DOUTE, rien n'est plus naturel ...

Ces quelques indications donnent PEUT-ETRE une idée suffisante de notre cité. AU DEMEURANT, ON NE DOIT RIEN EXAGERER. Ce qu'il fallait souligner, c'est l'aspect banal de la ville et de la vie. Mais on passe ses journées sans difficulté aussitôt qu'on a des habitudes. Du moment que notre ville favorise les habitudes, ON PEUT DIRE que tout est pour le mieux. SOUS CET ANGLE, SANS DOUTE, la vie n'est pas très passionnante. DU MOINS, on ne connaît pas chez nous le désordre ... MAIS IL EST JUSTE D'AJOUTER ... (I, 1219)

This whole passage can be seen to furnish a mirror reflection of the diffidence and distrust with which the narrator himself handles language in recounting, among other things, the story of Joseph Grand.

We have here then an example of textual autorepresentation, a phenomenon Jean Ricardou has described in these terms: 'Avec l'*autoreprésentation* ... il y aura bien effets de représentation mais au lieu de
renvoyer vers toujours autre chose, c'est le texte lui-même qu'ils
concernent, selon parfois des subtilités étranges, à différents
niveaux.'[3] Now, if what is reflected in the portrait of Grand were the
words of Rieux uttered during the course of the events recounted, we
would have an example of what Ricardou has defined as 'horizontal
autorepresentation' where 'tels aspects de la fiction, dans la mesure
où ils se lient d'un nombre excessif de ressemblances, tendent à se
représenter réciproquement,'[4] for then the two passages in question
would be situated on the same level of the text: that of the fiction.
(This was the case of the first reflection noted above between the
portrait of Grand and the account of the particular rôle of telegrams
and letters during the plague.) However, this is not the case here,
since the first passage concerning Grand, one of the *characters of the
fiction*, pointed to or reflected the narrative level of the text, Rieux's
discourse in his rôle as story-teller. Hence, the phenomenon is rather
that of 'vertical autorepresentation' characterized by the situation
where 'tels aspects de la fiction, paysage décrit, situation offerte,
idéologie proposée, s'efforcent de ressembler, selon ses manières,
à tels aspects de la narration qui les produit.'[5] Ricardou goes on to
point out that of the different forms of 'vertical autorepresentation,' it
is precisely the 'mise-en-abyme' that is 'l'une des occurences les mieux
visibles de ce dispositif.'[6] In addition to the mirroring process of autorepresentation, however, any *mise-en-abyme* also implies the existence
of a particular kind of relationship between the elements of the text
thus brought together: it is the same relationship that exists between
the microcosm and the macrocosm, the smaller element being contained within the larger one. This condition is naturally fulfilled with
regard to the relationship between a component of the fiction (the
character traits of Joseph Grand) and a feature of the narrative (the
language of Rieux as chronicler).

An analogous device can be seen at work in another passage concerning Grand. The difference lies in the fact that this time it does not
refer to other specific elements of the text, in other words to other
particular passages elsewhere in the novel. Rather it seems to point to
the very origins of the text in its entirety:

Rieux comprit seulement que l'œuvre en question avait déjà beaucoup de pages, mais que la peine que son auteur prenait pour l'amener à la perfection lui était très douloureuse. 'Des soirées, des semaines entières sur un mot ... et quelquefois une simple conjonction'... Les mots sortaient en trébuchant de sa bouche mal garnie.

— Comprenez bien, Docteur. A la rigueur, c'est assez facile de choisir entre mais *et* et. *C'est déjà plus difficile d'opter entre* et *et* puis. *La difficulté grandit avec* puis *et* ensuite. *Mais, assurément, ce qu'il y a de plus difficile c'est de savoir s'il faut mettre* et *ou s'il ne faut pas.* (I, 1301)

It would doubtless be equally pertinent to speak here either in more traditional critical terms of a kind of allegory of novelistic creation or of an *intratextual* allegory of the production of the text itself whereby the surface of the latter reveals here and there the traces of its own generation.

The text not only proffers a reflection of the generative process by which it has come to exist but at other points where it is again a question of Grand's activities as a writer, it points out its own present existence as a material object:

Dans la salle à manger, Grand l'invita [Rieux] à s'asseoir devant une table pleine de papiers couverts de ratures sur une écriture microscopique ...

[Grand]... contemplait toutes ces feuilles et sa main parut invinciblement attirée par l'une d'elles qu'il éleva en transparence devant l'ampoule électrique sans abat-jour. La feuille tremblait dans sa main, Rieux remarqua que le front de l'employé était moite. (I, 1301-2)

The text thus draws attention to the medium of paper and ink which provides the tangible form that constitutes it as an object of perception. And since in this respect, by virtue of the nature of its material existence, the printed page of *La Peste* in no wise differs from the original manuscript page, the text thus designates through this self-same gesture and by means of the very same passage the conditions of its own production:

d'une voix étrangement creuse, [Grand] les pria de lui apporter le manuscrit qu'il avait mis dans un tiroir. Tarrou lui donna les feuilles qu'il serra contre lui, sans les regarder, pour les tendre ensuite au docteur, l'invitant du geste à les lire. C'était un court manuscrit d'une cinquantaine de pages. Le docteur le feuilleta et comprit que toutes ces feuilles ne portaient que la même phrase indéfiniment recopiée, remaniée, enrichie ou appauvrie. Sans arrêt, le mois de mai, l'amazone et les allées du Bois se confrontaient et se disposaient de façons diverses. L'ouvrage comportait aussi des explications, parfois démesurément longues, et des variantes. Mais à la fin de la dernière page, une main appliquée avait seulement écrit, d'une encre fraîche: 'Ma bien chère Jeanne, c'est aujourd'hui Noël ...' Au-dessus, soigneusement calligraphiée, figurait la dernière version de la phrase. 'Lisez,' disait Grand. Et Rieux lut.

'Par une belle matinée de mai, une svelte amazone, montée sur une somptueuse jument alezane, parcourait, au milieu des fleurs, les allées du Bois ...' (I, 1432)

This last sentence, the object of Joseph Grand's unending care and attention, is itself, as I remarked in Chapter 1, a *mise-en-abyme* of the process of *énonciation* on the level of the generation of the whole text in which it is embedded. However, it functions thus in two complementary ways: both diachronically and synchronically. Through its recurrence in ever so slightly modified forms (no less than four: cf. I, 1302, 1327, 1328, and 1432), it reflects the actual historical emergence of the manuscript that was to become the text we have before us through the series of modifications and rewritings that it underwent, as though laying out before the reader's gaze the very variants which are normally effaced one after another and finally obscured forever beneath the definitive version of the text. It is as though it were openly to exhibit syntagmatically the various levels of the palimpsest that was the original manuscript, much in the manner of the French New Novel, such as Robbe-Grillet's *La Jalousie* for example, where the same passage recurs time and again but each time in a slightly modified form. In this sense, the diachronic, historical genesis of the text is made present and perceptible in its entirety, in other words synchronically, or, to change registers, the temporal is thereby transposed into the spatial. However, this sentence can at the same time be seen to function on a solely synchronic level, completely within the spatial dimension of the text without regard for its historical origins. For it also has all the appearance of a *mise-en-abyme* of the whole text within which it is contained and which it reproduces and *re*presents in miniature, just as the microcosm mirrors the macrocosm. I shall return later to the status and functioning of the *texts* within the *text*. What is, for me, beyond dispute is that it is possible to read the commentary Grand makes on his own sentence as a commentary on the language that goes to make up the text of *La Peste*, a language that never stops pointing itself out, drawing attention to itself instead of to the fiction that is its ostensible raison d'être:

– Ce n'est là qu'une approximation. Quand je serai arrivé à rendre parfaitement le tableau que j'ai dans l'imagination, quand ma phrase aura l'allure même de cette promenade au trot, une-deux-trois, une-deux-trois, alors le reste sera plus facile et surtout l'illusion sera telle, dès le début, qu'il sera possible de dire: 'Chapeau bas!'

Mais, pour cela, il avait encore du pain sur la planche. Il ne consentirait jamais à livrer cette phrase telle quelle à un imprimeur. Car, malgré le contentement qu'elle lui donnait parfois, il se rendait compte qu'ELLE NE COLLAIT PAS TOUT A FAIT ENCORE A LA REALITE ... (I, 1302-3)

The language of *La Peste* is no more effective than that of its character Grand in 'sticking' to the fictive reality it is intended to refer to and the illusion of which all the devices of autorepresentation serve to denounce.

Let us now leave aside all the various forms of autorepresentation we have been concerned with thus far and concentrate on one of them in particular: the *mise-en-abyme* in its most obvious and least debatable form. I am referring to the *mise-en-abyme* that is brought about by the particular organization of the different levels of the text: narration and fiction. (Here I retain Jean Ricardou's own terminology: 'Il est clair que la narration est la manière de raconter, la fiction ce qui est conté ...'⁷) The resulting structure is responsible for the text's taking on the appearance of a nest of boxes each fitting into a larger, identical version of itself like those popular Russian dolls. This will entail an examination of the over-all structure of the work as well as, although incidentally, the specific traits of its narrative technique.

The narrator presents his story as a chronicle, as I remarked at the beginning of this chapter:

Arrivé là, on admettra sans peine que rien ne pouvait faire espérer à nos concitoyens les incidents qui se produisirent au printemps de cette année-là et qui furent, nous le comprîmes ensuite, comme les premiers signes de la série des graves événements dont on s'est proposé de faire ici la chronique. Ces faits paraîtront bien naturels à certains et, à d'autres, invraisemblables au contraire. Mais, après tout, un chroniqueur ne peut tenir compte de ces contradictions. Sa tâche est seulement de dire: 'Ceci est arrivé,' lorsqu'il sait que ceci est, en effet, arrivé ... (I, 1219)

What cannot fail to strike the reader is the impersonal, almost anonymous tone of voice of the speaker, a characteristic which is perfectly in keeping, I might add, with the objectivity and neutrality sought after by the writer of a chronicle:

Du reste, le narrateur qu'on connaîtra toujours à temps, n'aurait guère de titre à faire valoir dans une entreprise de ce genre si le hasard ne l'avait mis à même de recueillir un certain nombre de dépositions et si la force des choses ne l'avait mêlé à tout ce qu'il prétend relater. C'est ce qui l'autorise à faire œuvre d'historien. Bien entendu, un historien, même s'il est un amateur, a toujours des documents. Le narrateur de cette histoire a donc les siens: son témoignage d'abord, celui des autres ensuite, puisque, par son rôle, il fut amené à recueillir les confidences de tous les personnages de cette chronique, et, en dernier lieu, les textes qui finirent par tomber entre ses mains. (I, 1219-20)

Almost identical terms will be used subsequently by the narrator when he comes to present another document that will play an important rôle in his own narrative and long extracts of which will, moreover, be incorporated therein. I am referring to Tarrou's diary:

le narrateur croit utile de donner sur la période qui vient d'être décrite l'opinion d'un autre témoin. Jean Tarrou, qu'on a déjà recontré au début de ce récit, s'était fixé à Oran quelques semaines plus tôt ...

Ses carnets ... constituent eux aussi une sorte de chronique de cette période difficile. Mais il s'agit d'une chronique très particulière qui semble obéir à un parti pris d'insignifiance ... Dans le désarroi général, il s'appliquait, en somme, à se faire l'historien de ce qui n'a pas d'histoire. On peut déplorer sans doute ce parti pris et y soupçonner la sécheresse du cœur. Mais il n'en reste pas moins que ces carnets peuvent fournir, pour une chronique de cette période, une foule de détails secondaires qui ont cependant leur importance et dont la bizarrerie même empêchera qu'on juge trop vite cet intéressant personnage. (I, 1233-4)

It is to be noted that Tarrou's diary is just as much a 'chronicle' as Rieux's tale, that the former too undertakes the work of a historian even if, in his case, he is not the historian of the 'graves événements' (I, 1219) the narrator speaks of but the historian 'de ce qui n'a pas d'histoire.' and finally, that his diary can give the impression of a certain 'sécheresse du cœur' that could also have been created by the objectivity and detachment of the narrator.

Tarrou's diary is, of course, just one of the 'documents' or 'texts' in the narrator's possession which enable him to 'faire œuvre d'historien.' (I, 1220) Moreover, the reader is not allowed to lose sight of its status as a document as he reads this narrative within the first narrative, this 'chronique' (I, 1234) within that other 'chronique' (I, 1219) that is *La Peste*. The material existence of the diary is constantly evoked: 'A vrai dire, ces carnets deviennent assez bizarres à partir du moment où les statistiques commencent à baisser. Est-ce la fatigue, mais L'ECRITURE EN DEVIENT DIFFICILEMENT LISIBLE et l'on passe trop souvent d'un sujet à l'autre.' (I, 1443) The passages quoted from the diary are often accompanied by the presentation of the actual document as well as by a commentary on its contents:

Ce sont les seuls endroits où les notes du voyageur, à cette date, semblent prendre un caractère personnel. Il est difficile simplement d'en apprécier la signification et le sérieux. C'est ainsi qu'après avoir relaté que la découverte d'un rat mort avait poussé le caissier de l'hôtel à commettre une erreur dans sa note, Tarrou avait ajouté, D'UNE ECRITURE MOINS NETTE QUE D'HABITUDE: 'Question: comment faire pour ne pas perdre son temps? Réponse: l'éprouver dans toute sa longueur. Moyens ...' Mais tout de suite après ces écarts de langage ou de pensée, les carnets entament une description détaillée des tramways ... et terminent ces considérations par un 'c'est remarquable' qui n'explique rien.' (I, 1235-6)

These sheets of writing that make up the second level of narrative of the text reproduce, through the by now familiar process of *mise-en-abyme*, the material reality of the latter:

Ici, du reste, l'écriture de Tarrou donnait des signes bizarres de fléchissement. Les lignes qui suivaient étaient difficilement lisibles et, comme pour donner une nouvelle preuve de ce fléchissement, les derniers mots étaient les premiers qui fussent personnels: 'Ma mère était ainsi, j'aimais en elle le même effacement et c'est elle que j'ai toujours voulu rejoindre. Il y a huit ans, je ne peux pas dire qu'elle soit morte. Elle s'est seulement effacée un peu plus que d'habitude et, quand je me suis retourné, elle n'était plus là.' (I, 1444)

The material existence of the diary is situated in that fictive universe that is the subject of the narrative (of the first narrator, that is), being just one of the documents the narrator has collected: 'Rentré chez lui, Tarrou rapportait cette scène et aussitôt (L'ECRITURE LE PROUVAIT ASSEZ) notait sa fatigue.' (I, 1447) This means that the level of the text corresponding to the diary belongs to the world of the fiction, whereas in relation to the events of Tarrou's everyday existence evoked in the diary's pages, on the other hand, it constitutes a second level of narration.

What we have here, is, if not the beginning, the potential for a new process of *mise-en-abyme*, the first consisting, as we have just seen, of the quotations from Tarrou's diary. This possibility is brought about by the fact that Tarrou's diary, in its turn, quotes other documents so that, just as the extracts from the latter are embedded within the larger text for which Rieux is responsible and which it, at the same time, mirrors due to the diary's status as a 'chronicle' within a 'chronicle,' so the written sources quoted by Tarrou are embedded in the text in which they figure. If I speak here of the 'potential' for the generation of a *mise-en-abyme* rather than its actual realization, it is because the actual situation where one text lies embedded does not, in itself, bring about or necessitate any mirroring effect as such on the part of the embedded text of the text that contains it. Unless, of course, one were to consider the common status as text of the two elements concerned as constituting a common identity that would justify considering the smaller the reflection of the larger. Such is clearly implied in the image of a microcosm/macrocosm relationship that I evoked in connection with the functioning of Joseph Grand's sentence on the synchronic level of the text as a spatial rather than a temporal phenomenon. Here it appears more reasonable, however, to postulate quite simply a situation of *enchâssement* where the vehicle of the first *enchâssement*, Tarrou's diary, becomes the framework for a second analogous embedding process[8] featuring further documents: hence, texts within a text within a text.

This is precisely the structuring effect analysed by Tzvetan Todorov in his essay 'Les Hommes-récits' on *A Thousand and One Nights* in *Poétique de la prose*. To the rhetorical question: 'Mais quelle est la signification interne de l'enchâssement ...?,' this theoretician replies: 'La structure du récit nous en fournit la réponse: l'enchâssement est une mise en évidence de la propriété la plus essentielle de tout récit. Car le récit enchâssant, c'est le *récit d'un récit*.' For present purposes, it suffices to read the term *text* where Todorov writes 'récit': 'En racontant l'histoire d'un autre récit, le premier atteint son thème fondamental et en même temps se réfléchit dans cette image de soi-même; le récit enchâssé est à la fois l'image de ce grand récit abstrait dont tous les autres ne sont que des parties infimes, et aussi du récit enchâssant qui le précède directement. Etre le récit d'un récit, c'est le sort de tout récit, qui se réalise à travers l'enchâssement.'[9] It is in this way that the process of reflection comes into play once again in the final analysis. Texts-within-texts here joins up with texts-about-texts, which provided the starting point of this chapter.

In the same manner, then, that Tarrou's diary figures among the 'documents' gathered together by the chronicler Rieux, other documents take their place *within* the diary like so many microtexts within the macrotext that contains them. Among their number, we find newspaper items, whether they have the brevity of headlines: '[des vendeurs de journaux] se répandront dans toute la ville, tendant à bout de bras les feuilles où éclate le mot "Peste". "Y aura-t-il un automne de peste? Le professeur B. répond: Non".' (I, 1314) Or reproduce the actual text of an article:

il s'est créé un autre journal: Le Courrier de l'épidémie, *qui se donne pour tâche d'"informer nos concitoyens, dans un souci de scrupuleuse objectivité, des progrès et des reculs de la maladie; de leur fournir les témoignages les plus autorisés sur l'avenir de l'épidémie; de prêter l'appui de ses colonnes à tous ceux, connus ou inconnus, qui sont disposés de lutter contre le fléau; de soutenir le moral de la population, de transmettre les directives des autorités et, en un mot, de grouper toutes les bonnes volontés pour lutter efficacement contre le mal qui nous frappe.'* (I, 1314)

At one point, we actually come across a third 'chronicle' that therefore figures as a chronicle within a chronicle within a chronicle! 'La chronique locale ... est maintenant occupée tout entière par une campagne contre la municipalité: "Nos édiles se sont-ils avisés du danger que pouvaient présenter les cadavres putréfiés de ces rongeurs?"' (I, 1237) Certain microtexts are also to be found in the form of signs:

Toutes les boutiques sont fermées. Mais sur quelques-unes, l'écriteau 'Fermé pour cause de peste' atteste qu'elles n'ouvriront pas tout à l'heure avec les autres.
(I, 1314)

Il n'y a pas longtemps, certains restaurants affichaient: 'Ici, le couvert est ébouillanté.' (I, 1315)

The preceding texts are therefore doubly embedded or framed as texts within a text within a text. If we now retrace our footsteps, so to speak, back to the point where the first level of *enchâssement* is produced by the various extracts from Tarrou's diary in the form of an actual *mise-en-abyme*, we notice that the latter document is itself surrounded by other documents which are also the object of the same *enchâssement* while not, for the reasons given earlier, creating a *mise-en-abyme*. These other texts, in addition to Joseph Grand's sentence, are of many kinds. Here, too, there are newspaper items:

La réponse du préfet en présence des critiques dont la presse se faisait l'écho ('Ne pourrait-on envisager un assouplissement des mesures envisagées?') fut assez imprévue. (I, 1280)

A les lire [les journaux], ce qui caractérisait la situation, c'était 'l'exemple émouvant de calme et de sang-froid' que donnait la population. (I, 1411)

But there are also posters: 'un mot d'ordre avait fini par courir qu'on lisait, parfois, sur les murs ... "Du pain ou de l'air".' (I 1411) Signs found in the windows of commercial establishments: 'Un café ayant affiché que "le vin tue le microbe," l'idée déjà naturelle au public que l'alcool préservait des maladies infectueuses se fortifia dans l'opinion.' (I, 1282) Not to mention official communiqués:

Le communiqué ajoutait, il est vrai, que dans un esprit de prudence qui ne pouvait manquer d'être approuvé par la population, les portes de la ville resteraient fermées pendant deux semaines encore et les mesures prophylactiques maintenues pendant un mois. Durant cette période, au moindre signe que le péril pouvait reprendre, 'le statu quo *devait être maintenu et les mesures reconduites au-delà.'* (I, 1440-1)

Also in the administrative domain is the hospital card that records Father Paneloux's death: 'On inscrivit sur la fiche: "Cas douteux".' (I, 1408) The postal services also provide other texts such as the official dispatch received by the Préfet: 'Bernard Rieux regardait la dépêche officielle que le préfet lui avait tendue ... La dépêche portait: "Déclarez l'état de peste. Fermez la ville".' (I, 1267) And the telegram Rambert sends to his wife in Paris: 'Il avait fini, après une attente de deux heures dans une file, par faire accepter un télégramme où il avait inscrit: "Tout va bien. A bientôt".' (I, 1285) It is perhaps even less surprising to find an extract from a medical handbook: 'une phrase revenait au docteur Rieux, une phrase qui terminait justement dans son manuel l'énumération des symptômes: "Le pouls devient filiforme et la mort survient à l'occasion d'un mouvement insignifiant".' (I, 1247) Nor should we overlook here the macabre text scrawled on Cottard's door announcing his intended suicide: 'sur la porte de gauche, Rieux lut, tracé à la craie rouge: "Entrez, je suis pendu".' (I, 1229)

Having analysed this two-tiered framing device of a frame within a frame where the element reflected contains the element reflecting and both, whether they constitute narrative or fiction, consist of texts (that is to say passages marked off by quotation marks), we must now come back to the interrelationship of the different levels of the text taken as a whole, as formal entities, in other words the over-all structure of *La Peste*.

At first sight, we appear to be confronted by a formal device that is, to all intents and purposes, the same as that just described: the dimension of the fiction dependent upon the narration of the first narrator takes on, in its turn, a narrative function in the shape of Tarrou's diary or even, theoretically, Grand's manuscript. But let us return once again to the first level of narrative, that for which the narrator of the whole chronicle is responsible: 'Cependant, avant d'entrer dans le détail de ces nouveaux événements, le narrateur croit utile de donner sur la période qui vient d'être décrite l'opinion d'un autre témoin.' (I, 1233) There appears to be no doubt of the narrative character, and solely narrative character, of this level of the text. Yet, at the beginning of the last chapter, we encounter a most curious phenomenon: 'Cette chronique touche à sa fin. Il est temps que le docteur Rieux avoue qu'il en est l'auteur.' (I, 1466) It consists of the unexpected appearance of what can only be described as a *pre-narrator*.[10] 'Le narrateur' is the creation of this prenarrator, whose existence endows even the level of the first narrator's narrative with a *fictive* status, since the person designated as 'le narrateur' is none other than a fictive character invented by Dr Rieux for his own purposes, that is to say to take on the rôle of story-teller.

The presence of a prenarrator was, in fact, already perceptible long before the last chapter of the novel. First of all, the designation of the narrator in the third person already implied the existence of some such unidentified and unmentioned person:

Car il faut bien parler des enterrements et LE NARRATEUR s'en excuse. IL sent bien le reproche qu'on pourrait LUI faire à cet égard, mais SA seule justification est qu'il y eut des enterrements pendant toute cette époque et que, d'une certaine manière, on L'a obligé ... à SE préoccuper des enterrements. Ce n'est pas, en tout cas, qu'IL ait du goût pour ces sortes de cérémonies ... (I, 1357)

Secondly, the narrative at times had recourse to a curiously ambiguous pronoun, the impersonal, third-person pronoun *on*: 'A ce point du récit qui laisse Bernard Rieux derrière sa fenêtre, ON permettra au narrateur de justifier l'incertitude et la surprise du docteur, puisque, avec des nuances, sa réaction fut celle de nos concitoyens.' (I, 1245)

What is strange here – and this emerges very clearly from the last passage quoted – is that the prenarrator, Rieux, the protagonist in the fight against the plague, who has created the character of 'le narrateur,' exists paradoxically on the level of the fiction as one of the characters involved in the events recounted. If Tarrou's diary constitutes, as we have seen, a first level of fiction, it is to the subsequent and last fictive dimension of the text that the prenarrator necessarily belongs: the series of events that are recounted by Tarrou as well as by Rieux. The one level of the text that appeared to be solely narrative in character (since that corresponding to Tarrou's diary constitutes a narrative *and* a fiction) finally proves to be dependent upon the fiction that was of its own creation. Thus, the tables have been turned and a logically impossible situation has arisen where the narrative has become the fiction and vice versa. The narrator turns out to be an invention of one of the characters whose story we have been following thanks to this imaginary intermediary without whose words the character would not have existed in the first place. What this means, in the final analysis, is that the prenarrator, although his name is finally revealed to us, Bernard Rieux, is wholly inaccessible and unknowable. Since the only Bernard Rieux known to us is the daily fighter against the plague, the companion-in-arms, so to speak, of Tarrou, Grand, and the rest of them. He is, moreover, only known to us from the outside,[11] his inner thoughts and feelings only perceptible inasmuch as they are articulated or given bodily expression. Even the ubiquitous and ambiguous narrative *on* does not describe his physical appearance directly but, instead, cites the portrait given in Tarrou's diary:

A titre documentaire, on peut enfin reproduire le portrait du docteur Rieux par Tarrou. Autant que le narrateur puisse juger, il est assez fidèle:
'Paraît trente-cinq ans. Taille moyen. Les épaules fortes. Visage presque rectangulaire. Les yeux sombres et droits, mais les mâchoires saillantes. Le nez fort est régulier. Cheveux noirs coupés très courts. La bouche est arquée avec des lèvres pleines et presque toujours serrées. Il a un peu l'air d'un paysan sicilien avec sa peau cuite, son poil noir et ses vêtements de teintes toujours foncées, mais qui lui vont bien.' (I, 1238)

The resulting narrative perspective is, when viewed retrospectively by the reader in the light of Rieux's revelation in the final chapter, not unlike that of *L'Etranger*. Bernard Rieux, like Meursault, speaks of himself as though he were another (except that in his case, it is as though the speaker, rather than the person spoken about, were another). And just as the narrator of *La Chute* will assume the rôle of a certain Jean-Baptiste Clamence, judge-penitent and false prophet, in order to trap his listener, so the narrator of *La Peste* assumes a false identity for the purposes of his narration. It is difficult not to perceive in the relationship between these three novelistic texts of Camus variations on a common theme: ostensibly of masks and men, of stories and story-tellers or, more pertinently for the present context, of mirrors and mirages. Characters who refuse to identify themselves are produced by texts that never stop doing so.

What this amounts to in terms of narrative structure is that the story within a story within a story constituted by the events of the plague recounted by Tarrou and then subsequently recounted yet again by the narrator of the chronicle entitled *La Peste* is taken one stage further and thereby circles back upon itself. For one of the protagonists of the story of the events of the plague is, in fact, the creator of the first narrator and hence, in the final analysis, responsible for the latter's narrative. Now, if, as we have seen, each level of fiction is *enchâssé* or framed by the narrative level which it is dependent upon for its existence, the outer and first framework (the first level of narrative) ends up by being framed by that which is the object of the second framing process (Tarrou's diary), that is by the fiction. The story of Rieux and his fellow citizens is contained within Tarrou's narrative which is contained within 'the narrator''s narrative for which Rieux is responsible. The process of *enchâssement* has been turned inside out like a glove.[12]

What more fitting an image of autorepresentation could there be than this remarkable structure wherein each level of the text is *enchâssé* by and embedded within the preceding level and each level functions both as a narrative and a fiction? The final twist whereby this movement of *enchâssement*, having renewed itself once, then turns back upon itself, like the proverbial snake that eats its own tail/tale, so that the repetition could, theoretically, be repeated ad infinitum, brings to mind the 'jeu de glaces étudié' evoked in the 'Prière d'insérer' of *La Chute*, the 'glaces' corresponding here to the different levels of the text. Thus, in *La Peste*, all and every fiction is endlessly undermined by the manner in which the text never ceases to refer to itself and to proclaim its status as text. As Sylvère Lotringer has put it, 'l'*autoreprésentation* subvertit le jeu de la représentation en le prenant, si l'on peut dire, au mot: si l'on ne peut barrer entièrement l'effet référentiel, qui est inscrit dans le langage, on peut lui-même le représenter, en d'autres termes ... le détourner et contourner afin de le renvoyer au texte même.'[13]

The Self-Generating Text:
'Jonas'

In this chapter, I shall be looking at a different form of narcissism from that operative in *La Peste*. The *textual* narcissism of the latter novel will give way to the *linguistic* narcissism that can be seen at work within the very texture of the text as it spins itself out in a process of autogeneration, continually mirroring itself so that production and reproduction become synonymous.

The short story 'Jonas ou l'artiste au travail' concludes with an enigma which, in the context of the tale that precedes it, is tantamount to a pun, that is to say a play on words. There is, in fact, only one word, but that word can be read as one of two alternatives. It is 'un mot qu'on pouvait déchiffrer, mais dont on ne savait s'il fallait y lire *solitaire* ou *solidaire*.' (I, 1652) The two spellings of the word sum up so well the two polarities of Camus' whole literary output – a dichotomy that is to be found in all he wrote and that is reflected in the very titles of his texts: *L'Envers et l'endroit*, 'Entre oui et non,' *L'Exil et le royaume* – that one might well suspect that in this play on words lies the very raison d'être of this short story. The opposition between solitude and solidarity, the two 'temptations' Camus was continually confronted with, stands out here in such sharp relief that the whole of the text could be nothing more than a pretext to obtain this final effect. That being so, it should come as no surprise to discover that the text that serves as a mere pretext for a play on words[1] should itself prove to be the product of a play on words. The text would thereby turn out to be the occasion and place for play, like the apartment it describes where beings 'semblaient flotter comme des ludions dans un aquarium vertical.' (I, 1633)

The text begins thus: 'Gilbert Jonas, artiste peintre, croyait en son étoile.' (I, 1627) Where has this star come from? It was already to be found in Camus' *Carnets* on 10 January 1950: 'Je n'ai jamais vu très clair en moi pour finir. Mais j'ai toujours suivi, d'instinct, une étoile invisible.'[2] In 1958, in reply to a questionnaire presented to him by a North American academic, Camus speaks of experiencing 'le senti-ment d'une "étoile" particulière.'[3] It should moreover be pointed out that one of the possible sources of this short story is an essay by Henry Miller entitled *Un Etre étoilique*.[4]

Jonas attributes the 'succès' (I, 1642) that he meets with in the eyes of the critics to his star: 'Jonas rendait justice à son étoile plutôt qu'à ses mérites.' (I, 1627) He accounts for the monthly retainer paid to him by the art dealer in the same way: 'Jonas en lui-même remerciait son étoile ... "Ça, disait-il, c'est une chance!" Il pensait en réalité: "C'est une chance qui continue." Aussi loin qu'il pût remonter dans sa mémoire, il trouvait cette chance a l'œuvre.' (I, 1627) In other words, what is at work here is none other than his star, which is responsible not only for his success but also for the text itself. This is hardly surprising since, according to the Robert Dictionary, 'l'étoile' is 'un astre producteur et emetteur d'énergie.' Let us now consider what is produced by 'l'étoile.'

What 'l'étoile' produces in the first place is 'la production de Jonas' (I, 1638): 'les toiles' that Jonas works on. And it is only to be expected that his 'toiles' are often mentioned in the text. It goes with-out saying that the word 'tableau' also derives from 'l'étoile' by semantic association. What is less obvious is the analogous genesis of the 'carré du ciel dessiné par la cour' (I, 1635) against the back-ground of which the daylight was fading away as Jonas decided to lay down his paintbrush and the shape of which reproduces that of the canvas ('toile') the artist was seated in front of. But its genesis is doubly determined by the fact that it is within the 'carré du ciel' that 'l'étoile' will subsequently appear.

The production of his 'toiles' under the influence of his 'étoile' makes of Jonas himself a star. For 'le succès de Jonas lui valut' not only 'des amis' (1634) but also '[des] disciples' (1636) and he thus becomes the 'maître' (1636) of a school of painting: 'Jonas main-tenant faisait école.' (1636) Indeed, with the changing of a conso-nant and the dropping of a vowel, *étoile* becomes *école*. But let us return to the 'maître,' a term that is inevitably called forth by 'école.' Nowhere could one find a kinder nor more helpful master. 'Ce sera comme vous voudrez' (1627, 1632, 1634, 1639, 1650) is the refrain with which he greets every call on his services, every request for help. One can appreciate that his wife Louise does indeed 'se sais[ir] d'un mètre pliant' (1638) and well before she needs it to measure their apartment. For it was on the occasion of their marriage that she got her hands on a master who would do all that was asked of him and put up with anything.

The star is normally to be found within its constellation. Jonas the star is no exception to this rule since he paints away surrounded by a constellation of attentive faces: 'Ainsi coulait le temps de Jonas, qui peignait au milieu d'amis et d'élèves, installés sur des chaises maintenant disposées en rangs concentriques autour du chevalet.' (1637) If the word *constellation* does not itself figure in the text, it is as though it were conjured up by its phonetic half-brother 'installation,' in which one can hear its echo. The noun 'installation' appears four times (1631 and 1633), as does the verb 's'installer' (1630, 1634, 1638, 1646). 'Installation' produces, in its turn, 'organization' (1638, 1639, 1646) with its verbal form (1648), which brings us back to the original star thanks to the organization of the planetary system. In fact, the very way in which the teacups are passed around suggests the movement of the planets:

Les tasses passaient de main en main, parcouraient le couloir, de la cuisine à la grande pièce, revenaient ensuite pour atterrir dans le petit atelier où Jonas, au milieu d'une poignée d'amis et de visiteurs qui suffisaient à remplir la chambre, continuait de peindre jusqu'au moment où il devait déposer ses pinceaux pour prendre, avec reconnaissance, la tasse qu'une fascinante personne avait spécialement remplie pour lui. (1641)

But before systematically going through the inventory of all the vocabulary that belongs, by association, to the domain of the stars, I should point out that the image of the 'rangs concentriques' formed by the chairs the friends and disciples are occupying, an image that can be seen to represent in visual form the situation of the star, is not the only one of its kind. The description of the way in which Louise tries to enter Jonas's studio without disturbing him, stretching out her limbs in all directions at once and at the same time walking on tip-toe, 'sur la pointe des pieds' (1633), seems to reproduce the shape of the star from which the text originates. Nothing could be more visually striking by its very grotesqueness than this 'mimique où Louise, les bras largement écartés, le torse un peu renversé en arrière, et la jambe lancée très haut devant elle, ne pouvait pas passer inaperçue.' (1634)

A whole vocabulary is to be found arising from the existence of the sky or the cosmos. The revolution of the planets is associated with 'les toiles' (*l'étoile*) in the following sentence: 'ils mettaient au-dessus de tout les toiles de la première période, mais les recherches actuelles préparaient une véritable révolution.' (1639) The word 'voies' (1628) calls to mind the milky way (*la voie lactée*), just as 'croissance' (1638) is related to *croissant* or the crescent-shaped quarter-moon. Certain passages are particularly rich in this respect and allow us to trace the activity of the original star in some detail. In the following example, the verb 'cumuler' suggests a particular kind of cloud, the cumulus (*le cumulus*), while the dedication of the heavenly creature or 'ange' Louise shines forth in the manner of a star:

L'étoile décidément protégeait Jonas qui pouvait ainsi CUMULER sans mauvaise conscience les certitudes de la mémoire et les commodités de l'oubli.

Mais les trésors de dévouement que prodiguait Louise ETINCELAIENT DE LEURS PLUS BEAUX FEUX dans la vie quotidienne de Jonas. Ce bon ANGE lui évitait des achats de chaussures, de vêtements et de linge qui abrègent, pour tout homme normal, les jours d'une vie déjà si courte. (1630)

Later on in the text, 'cumuler' returns in the form of Jonas's correspondence, which 's'accumulait' (1641). The working-out of the star can be found in an even more succinct form on the level of a single sentence: 'Il fallait écarter les toiles, déplier la toile perfectionnée, et s'installer avec les petits.' (1634) In addition to the verb 's'installer,' mentioned earlier, we here see the line of derivation going from *étoile* to *toile* to *tableau* and thence to *table* with an *étoile* disseminated in 'é[carter les] toiles' and an incomplete *tableau* in 'table.'

There is not only the vocabulary of the text that is related either by phonetic or semantic association to the phenomenon of the sky. Certain images, apparently having no connection with the sky, reveal, on closer inspection, precisely the same association. Note, for example, that 'une ombre de tristesse' (1638) passes cloudlike over Louise's countenance. And when destiny no longer smiles on Jonas and his star no longer watches over him with its 'sourire bienveillant' (1629) so that he loses his 'naturelle bienveillance' (1637), our hero and his reputation begin to decline ('baiss[er],' 1642 and 1645) in harmony with the fading light from his star. Indeed he himself makes the connection between the sky and the star and, significantly, in a moment of discouragement, Jonas 'leva les yeux vers le ciel sans étoiles, et alla tirer les rideaux' (1643), as though losing all hope of bathing again in the inspirational light of his benevolent star. The more conscious he becomes of the difficulty he is experiencing in carrying on his painting as successfully as he had been wont to do, the more time he spends gazing at the sky as if looking for his absent star: 'Il était toujours assidu, mais il avait maintenant de la difficulté à peindre, même dans les moments de solitude. Ces moments, il les passait à regarder le ciel. Il avait toujours été distrait et absorbé, il devint rêveur. Il pensait à la peinture, à sa vocation, au lieu de peindre.' (1645) I shall return later to his 'solitude,' but the significance of his dream-like state is clear enough for had he not been in the habit of 'rêver à son étoile'? (1630) We can therefore understand why 'rêverie' (1628) plays such a large part in the story of Jonas (cf. also 1638 and 1646). And so, 'à cette époque, il peignait des ciels' (1645), as though seeking to conjure up the star he so sorely missed. It is, moreover, significant that at Louise's suggestion that he paint an 'ouvrière,' 'il essaya, gâcha deux toiles, puis revint à un ciel commencé.' (1646)

There is little need to stress the obvious relationship between *l'étoile* and light in general. Moreover, to a certain extent, the state of the sky and the amount of illumination are directly related. We read that 'l'appartement était littéralement violé par la lumière.' (1632) At the same time stress is also placed upon artificial lighting with the description of the 'système d'éclairage.' (1632) Although electric light has nothing to do with the sky, it does have something more directly in common with that other source of light, *l'étoile*, and that is its intensity. One finds in the imagery of the text a continual interplay between lightness and darkness, as in the following sentence where it is as though 'peinait' represented, on the level of both signifier and signified, a defective and incomplete form of *peignait*: 'Jonas qui peinait longuement pour recevoir de loin en loin une sorte d'éclair fugitif où la réalité surgissait alors à ses yeux dans une lumière vierge, n'avait qu'une idée obscure de sa propre esthétique.' (1636) It is clear that for Jonas himself darkness is brought about by the absence of the star: 'Il allait peindre, c'était sûr, et mieux peindre après cette période de vide apparent. Ça travaillait au-dedans, voilà tout, l'étoile sortirait lavée à neuf, étincelante, de ces brouillards obscurs.' (1647) Darkness attains its zenith, in both the astronomical and the general sense of the term, in the form of the attic that the frustrated artist builds for himself and in which he first of all remains 'immobile, dans l'obscurité, la journée entière.' (1650) What exactly does he do there?

il attendait son étoile, encore cachée, mais qui se préparait à monter de nouveau, à surgir enfin, inaltérable, au-dessus du désordre de ces jours vides. 'Brille, brille, disait-il. Ne me prive pas de ta lumière.' Elle allait briller de nouveau, il en était sûr. Mais il fallait qu'il réfléchît encore plus longtemps, puisque la chance lui était enfin donnée d'être seul sans se séparer des siens. (1650)

Note, in passing, the reappearance of the theme of solitude and also of the relatonship between the process of 'réflexion' (1638) which recurs at least seven times (1636, 1643, 1646, 1649) and the rôle of light originating from the star. If Jonas spends so much time reflecting, it is precisely under the influence of the rays of starlight.

When his friend Rateau asks Jonas what he is doing in his attic and Jonas replies that he is busy working or at least that it is 'tout comme,' the reader can very well mistake the word 'toile' for *étoile* in Rateau's reply: 'Mais tu n'as pas de toile!' (1651), says Rateau. The evening on which the latter finds the lamp lit in the attic for the first time coincides with the occasion when Jonas asks him for a canvas which his friend brings him. Thus the bringing of 'la toile' and the return of 'l'étoile' are contemporaneous, as is suggested by the fact that the artist had lit his lamp: 'La lampe resta allumée toute la nuit et toute la matinée du lendemain. A ceux qui venaient, Rateau ou Louise, Jonas répondait seulement: "Laisse, je travaille." A midi, il demanda du pétrole. La lampe, qui charbonnait, brilla de nouveau d'un vif éclat jusqu'au soir.' (1651) His artistic inspiration comes to life again in the presence of this 'vif éclat' which reveals that his star is once again watching over him. This lamp burning 'd'un vif éclat' recalls the 'trésors de dévouement,' manifested by Louise, which 'étincelaient de leurs plus beaux feux' (1630), as well as the way in which the virtue and disinterestedness of Louise's sister and niece 'éclataient dans leur nature honnête.' (1644) (This whole range of vocabulary, it should be added, can bring to mind the effects of a precious stone or diamond, to which I shall return later.)

Once his canvas has been completed, Jonas listens to the noise outside, 'la belle rumeur des hommes': 'De si loin elle ne contrariait pas cette force joyeuse en lui, son art, ces pensées qu'il ne pouvait pas dire, à jamais silencieuses, mais qui le mettaient au-dessus de toutes choses, dans un air libre et vif.' (1652) Here we can appreciate the ultimate realization of the expression of being placed 'au-dessus de toutes choses' like the star. The previous formulation of the same idea ('Tous, certainement, plaçaient très haut les travaux de l'artiste ...' [1635]; '[Ses disciples] le mettaient si haut dans leurs discours ... qu'après cela aucune faiblesse ne lui était permise.' [1636]) merely foretold the apotheosis by which he would see himself once and for all inhabiting the stellar regions. Proof of this is found in the fact that the star's light will survive the snuffing out of the lamp, which will, on the contrary, enable him the better to appreciate the renewed intensity of the star: 'Il éteignit la lampe et, dans l'obscurité revenue, là, n'était-ce pas son étoile qui brillait toujours? C'était elle, il la reconnaissait, le cœur plein de gratitude ...' (1652)

The interplay between light and dark which fulfils so significant a rôle in this text is paralleled by an even more marked phenomenon: the alternation between an opening-out and a narrowing-down of space. The status of the star as a symbol of expanding space is no less obvious than its rôle as a source of light. The original space, that of the young couple's apartment, is generous by virtue of its exceptionally vast dimensions, since the apartment, with its rooms that are 'particulièrement hautes,' 'offrait à ses hôtes un grand volume d'air' (1631), in spite of the fact that this 'important cubage d'air' had already been divided up horizontally, if not vertically, because 'les nécessités de l'entassement urbain et de la rente immobilière avaient contraint les propriétaires successifs à couper par des cloisons ces pièces trop vastes, et à multiplier par ce moyen les

stalles qu'ils louaient au prix fort à leur troupeau de locataires.'
(1631-2) With the birth of their children, the young couple find themselves 'contraint[s],' that is to say, short of usable living space:

*Le problème de l'espace vital l'emportait de loin ... sur les autres problèmes du
ménage, car le temps et L'ESPACE SE RETRECISSAIENT du même mouvement,
autour d'eux. La naissance des enfants, le nouveau métier de Jonas, leur
INSTALLATION ETROITE, et la modestie de la mensualité qui interdisait
d'acheter un plus grand appartement, ne laissaient qu'un CHAMP RESTREINT à
la double activité de Louise et de Jonas.* (1631)

Note the reappearance of the word 'installation' (out of *constellation*)
accompanied by the epithet 'étroite.' The latter word reveals that the
theme of ever-reducing space is doubly determined by *l'étoile*: first of
all, as we have seen, through the association of opposites (since the
star shines forth and thereby encroaches upon the surrounding space)
and secondly, through phonetic and lexical association. For through
the replacement of one consonant by another and the addition of a
further one, *étoile* produces 'étroite,' an adjective that occurs four
times in the text (cf. 1631, 1632, 1644, 1649).

Everywhere we find the cramped nature of space ('exiguité' [1633]
underlined, as in the case of the shower which 'pouvait en effet passer
passer pour tel[le] à la condition d'y installer un appareil, de le
placer dans le sens vertical et de consentir à recevoir le jet bienfaisant
dans une immobilité absolue' (1632-3) and the kitchen in which 'on
pouvait ... à la rigueur, manger ... pourvu que Jonas, ou Louise,
voulût bien se tenir debout.' (1633) This vertical 'jet bienfaisant,'
descending from on high, whose 'bienfaisan[ce],' through the 'bienveillance' noted earlier, is already related to the star that watches over
('veille') Jonas, as well as the purely vertical spaciousness of the rooms
gives the impression of a movement reaching up towards the source of
the starlight, laying way beyond a ceiling and a roof that already seem
far away:

*La hauteur vraiment extraordinaire des plafonds, et l'exiguité des pièces,
faisaient de cet appartement un étrange assemblage de parallélépipèdes presque
entièrement vitrés, tout en portes et en fenêtres, où les meubles ne pouvaient
trouver d'appui et où les êtres, perdus dans la lumière blanche et violent, semblaient flotter comme des ludions dans un aquarium vertical.* (1633)

The effect created here is not wholly dissimilar to the impression of human bodies floating in interplanetary space, where the force of terrestrial gravity no longer operates. The building itself is like an enormous contraption designed to attract and disseminate light while subjecting it to endlessly varying refractions and reflections: ' "C'est le cabinet des glaces," disait Jonas ravi.' (1633)

In spite of numerous 'installations ingénieuses' in the form of 'portes roulantes ... tablettes escamotables et ... tables pliantes' ('mètre pliant' gave us *maître pliant*), when 'les pièces furent pleines de tableaux et d'enfants, il fallait songer sans tarder à une nouvelle installation' (cf. *constellation*).(1633) And space continues to prove to be more and more at a premium as it rapidly dimishes. Thus, Louise 's'inquiétait devant la croissance de ses deux aînés et l'étroitesse de leur chambre.' (1638) She therefore puts them in the biggest room and Jonas moves into the little room with the baby, for, 'en raison de l'encombrement créé par ses toiles et celles de ses élèves, de beaucoup les plus nombreuses, il travaillait, ordinairement, dans un espace à peine plus grand que celui qui lui serait, désormais, attribué.' (1638) But even this set-up cannot last for long since 'l'enfant le gênait. Il grandissait d'ailleurs, il faudrait acheter un divan, qui prendrait de la place.' (1643) A new arrangement has therefore to be found: 'Jonas occupait la chambre conjugale et travaillait dans l'espace qui séparait le lit de la fenêtre.' (1644) As his friends and acquaintances continue to encroach upon his living and working space, the painter finds himself reduced to a final solution which will guarantee him a space that will be his alone even if it only furnishes a limited amount of room: 'Dans l'angle droit que faisaient les deux couloirs, il s'arrêta et considéra longuement les hauts murs qui s'élevaient jusqu'au plafond obscur ... A mi-hauteur des murs, il construisit un plancher pour obtenir une sorte de soupente étroite, quoique haute et profonde.' (1648-9) This last refuge, since it is situated high up below the ceiling, has the effect of bringing him closer to his star while at the same time ensuring his solitude.

'Solitude' (1645) also derives from *l'étoile* via its adjectival form 'solitaire' (1644, 1652), which generates a whole family of words that are either synonyms such as 'seul' (1650) and 'isolement' (1638) or else are very close in meaning while at the same time rhyming with 'solitaire' as in the case of 'singulière.' (1647) For 'solitaire' is also, as a noun, the name of a diamond which, like the star, 'étinc[èle] de [ses] plus beaux feux' (1630) and shines 'd'un vif éclat.' (1651) Through the rays of reflected light it throws forth, the diamond also suggests the shape of the star as seen from afar, in the sky. It is interesting to note that in a first tentative version of this text, a 'mimodrame en deux actes' entitled 'La Vie d'artiste,' we find a jeweller bringing Jonas 'des écrins' (jewel-cases) (2049) and later returning to reclaim possession of the 'bijoux' (2051). We can now appreciate how the play on words with which the text concludes '*solitaire* ou *solidaire*' is itself a product of the star 'à l'œuvre' (1628) for the last time, if only through the intermediary of another planet since the common denominator of 'solitaire' and 'solidaire' is none other than *solaire*. What is more, the effect created by the whole of this last sentence of the short story is of an even greater complexity and constitutes a résumé of the activity of the star – and not the artist – 'au travail.' It is an effect of duplication with the star as its object, a *mise-en-abyme* of 'l'étoile,' since the 'solitaire' (or star-like diamond) is located right in the middle of a wholly white '[é]toile': 'Dans l'autre pièce, Rateau regardait la toile, entièrement blanche, au centre de laquelle Jonas avait seulement écrit, en très petits caractères, un mot qu'on pouvait déchiffrer, mais dont on ne savait s'il fallait y lire *solitaire* ou *solidaire*.' (1652) This is then yet another of the 'bons effets de [l']étoile.' (1629)

What we have here is a fine example of what Jean Ricardou has called 'l'autoreprésentation,' where 'il y aura bien effets de représentation mais, au lieu de renvoyer vers toujours autre chose, c'est le texte lui-même qu'ils concernent, selon parfois des subtilités étranges, à différents niveaux.'[5] It comes as no surprise to discover, moreover, that this *texte-étoile* is a close cousin of Roland Barthes' 'texte étoilé'[6] and ends up like a spot of ink on blotting paper spreading out, star-like, in all directions to extend beyond its own confines as a text corresponding to the short story 'Jonas' and to participate in the process of what one might call, paradoxically, an internal or intra-intertextuality,[7] that is to say an intertextuality where the texts concerned are all part of the same writer's literary corpus.

The other texts that it thereby most ostensibly joins up with in a movement of reciprocal interplay are the two novels *L'Etranger* and *La Chute*. Thus Jonas's refrain 'Ce sera comme vous voudrez' echoes its textual variant, Meursault's equally characteristic response to all and sundry 'Cela m'était égal' so that each text can be read behind the other, so to speak, creating a kind of palempsestic effect that contributes to the internal textual dynamics of Camus' total writings or *œuvre* (an effect I shall return to later). More importantly, everything in this text which, at first sight, it does not appear possible to attribute to the 'astre producteur' tends, through the strongly ironical tone that it takes on, to echo or foreshadow (since historical chronology is not an operative concept on the level of textual production) those maxims which constitute the very substance of much of Clamence's narrative in *La Chute*. We read that 'L'étoile décidément protégeait Jonas qui pouvait ainsi cumuler sans mauvaise conscience les certitudes de la mémoire et les commodités de l'oubli' (1630), just as, for Clamence, the confession of the errors of his ways allows him 'de recommencer plus légèrement et de jouir deux fois, de [sa] nature d'abord, et ensuite d'un charmant repentir.' (1546) When the latter says: 'J'ai connu un cœur pur qui refusait la méfiance' (1479), it is as though he were referring to Jonas himself, of whom it is written: '"Nous n'avons rien à cacher," disait ce cœur pur.' (1632) The short story and the novel come together at several points, whether it be on the level of actual formulations:

'Il ne faut plus dire, affirmait Louise, qu'un tel est méchant ou laid, mais qu'il se veut méchant ou laid.' La nuance était importante et risquait de mener au moins ... à la condamnation du genre humain. ('Jonas,' 1629)

Chacun exige d'être innocent, à tout prix, même si, pour cela, il faut accuser le genre humain ... (*La Chute*, 1515)

Or whether it be on the level of character depiction: for just as Jonas has his 'étoile,' Clamence feels himself to be personally singled out for a success that is also written in the stars: 'à force d'être comblé, je me sentais ... désigné. Désigné personnellement, entre tous, pour cette longue et constante réussite.' (1488) Similarly, just as the artist accepts the friendship of others 'avec une simplicité encourageante' (1628), the judge-penitent accepts the homage paid to him by 'la vie, ses êtres et ses dons' 'avec une bienveillante fierté.' (1488) If the former is, as we have seen, placed 'si haut dans [les] discours' of his friends and disciples, the latter appears to be offering him his condolences when he exclaims: 'Le ciel nous préserve, cher Monsieur, d'être placé trop haut par nos amis!' (1489)

But let us return to the irony of the ironical overtones mentioned above. The story of the adultery committed by Jonas's father provides a fine example of this: 'il ne pouvait supporter les bonnes œuvres de sa femme, véritable sainte laïque ... le mari prétendait disposer en maître des vertus de sa femme. "J'en ai assez, disait cet OTHELLO, d'être trompé avec les pauvres".' (1628) Clamence has recourse to a similarly ironical nomenclature: 'Bien entendu, le véritable amour est exceptionnel, deux ou trois fois par siècle à peu près ... Pour moi, en tout cas, je n'étais pas la RELIGIEUSE PORTUGAISE.' (1503) But whereas Clamence appears to make fun of himself, for example, as a 'Français cartésien' (1513), the irony being exercised at his own expense, it is not Jonas who calls himself or even considers himself a 'cœur pur,' refusing thereby to take himself seriously, but an omniscient narrator (neither is it his father who takes himself for Othello). In fact, the text of this short story is unique in the Camusian canon precisely inasmuch as the irony exercised at the expense of the characters cannot possibly be attributed to the protagonist (as is, at least, possible in the second part of *L'Etranger* for example), if only because elsewhere (in *L'Etranger* and *La Chute*, in particular) the irony is accompanied by a first person narrative. Here, the characters and their lives are pictured by the reader at a certain distance, seen, if not from afar, certainly not as close to, as would be necessary for one to identify with them. (Perhaps the fact that the short story was preceded, genetically speaking, as mentioned earlier, by the play-form – and a silent one at that! – of the 'mimodrame' has something to do with this distancing effect which it can be seen thereby to 'account for' if not, of course, to 'explain' within the actual functioning of the final text.) It is clear that these characters are not intended to be taken too seriously. This is true even of Jonas himself. His misfortunes constitute a cautionary tale concerning the likely fate of the successful Parisian painter. That this tale was inspired by Camus' own bitter experience as a successful writer can be demonstrated readily enough by the following lines from a letter to a friend dated 15 February 1953:

La vérité est que je dispute au temps et aux êtres chaque heure de mon travail, sans y réussir, le plus souvent ... le plus grave est que je n'ai plus le temps, ni le loisir intérieur, d'écrire mes livres ... Depuis quelques années d'ailleurs, mon

œuvre ne m'a pas libéré, elle m'a asservi ... certains matins, lassé du bruit,
découragé devant l'œuvre interminable à poursuivre, malade de cette folie du
monde aussi qui vous assaille dans le journal, sûr enfin que je ne suffirai pas et
que je décevrai tout le monde, je n'ai que l'envie de m'asseoir et d'attendre que le
soir arrive. J'ai cette envie et j'y cède parfois. (1, 2054)

However, the heartfelt motivation underlying its genesis does not
make of Jonas, its protagonist, a tragic figure. Here the seeds of
tragedy are dissipated by the all-pervasive irony which intercedes
similarly in that most autobiographical of Camus' works, *La Chute*,
which constitutes, on one level and in its own peculiar fashion, a *confession* while precisely uttering a warning against any kind of confession,
literary or otherwise.

This cautionary tale in fact reads at times like one of Aesop's fables:

Selon RATeau, d'ailleurs, Louise ne méritait pas d'être regardée. Petit et râblé
lui-même, il n'aimait que les grandes femmes. 'Je ne sais pas ce que tu trouves
à cette FOURMI,' disait-il. Louise était en effet petite, noire de peau, de poils et
d'œil, mais bien faite, et de jolie mine. Jonas, grand et solide, s'attendrissait
sur la FOURMI, d'autant plus qu'elle était INDUSTRIEUSE. (1629)

Nothing could be further removed from any kind of realism than this
short story. All is seen at one remove, as though through the wrong
end of a telescope or, indeed, as if from the vantage point of another
planet – or star. Thus, *l'étoile* intervenes, in the final analysis, in the
very narrative process itself, determining the perspective it offers the
reader on the events related and the characters depicted. Is this not
yet another form of the autorepresentation we have already seen to be
at work, but of the *vertical* kind, as described by Jean Ricardou,
where 'tels aspects de la fiction, paysage décrit, situation offerte,
idéologie proposée, s'efforcent de ressembler, selon ses manières,
à tels aspects de la narration qui les produit'?[8]

Everything in this text, indeed, as Jonas says himself, 'est un effet
de l'étoile.' (1635) It is 'l'astre producteur,' to refer again to the
definition given by the Robert Dictionary, that has generated the
whole text. In the light, so to speak, of such a marked effect that the
star can be seen to have here, Rateau's words prove to have unexpected implications, when he says to Jonas: 'Ce ne sont pas tes

tableaux que j'aime. C'est ta peinture.' (1639) In a like manner, it is the process of *writing* that here prevails at the expense of the *work of art* seen as a static, immutable object fixed for all eternity in a sterile immobility, wholly comparable to the painting entitled *Ouvrière* that Jonas does not succeed in completing and that was to portray Rose's cousin sewing. It is significant that the very moment when Jonas 'qui peignait la donatrice aux chiens ... était peint lui-même par un artiste officiel' and when 'l'Artiste au travail' (1642) was consequently about to constitute the subject of someone else's painting, marks the beginning of the decline of Jonas's artistic ability when it is said by one of the art experts that Jonas 'baisse.' (1642) The pertinence of the fact that the actual text of the short story bears precisely the subtitle 'l'artiste au travail' becomes clear. What could more effectively draw attention to the text's refusal to accept to see itself transformed from an occasion and place for play into a work of art, in other words a consumer object? In other words, as Roland Barthes puts it, the text 'décante l'œuvre ... de sa consommation et la recueille comme jeu, travail, production, pratique.'[9] The opposition here is between product and production, the result and the process, as Barthes explains in the following terms:

l'œuvre est un fragment de substance, elle occupe une partie de l'espace des livres (par exemple dans une bibliothèque). Le texte lui est un champ méthodologique ... l'œuvre se tient dans la main, le texte se tient dans le langage ... L'œuvre se ferme sur un signifié ... Le texte, au contraire, pratique le recul infini du signifié, le texte est dilatoire; son champ est celui du signifiant ...[10]

I have accounted for the subtitle of the short story 'L'Artiste au travail,' but have said nothing to explain the title itself. Why 'Jonas'? The reason is not far to seek once one is alerted to the activity of the star. 'J'en ai assez, disait cet Othello (*le père de Jonas*), d'être trompé avec les pauvres' (1628), we read in the text. In other words, for the character in question, 'c'est assez.' It so happens that the name in French for one of the constellations is *CETACE*. And sure enough the constellation concerned is none other than that of the *whale* who swallowed up the luckless Jonas.

The Hermeneutic Paradigm:
L'Etranger

Let us look again at the sentence that concludes 'Jonas.' All appearances to the contrary, we have still not exhausted its implications. In addition to its autoreferential rôle on the level of the generation of the text, it also points to the other end of the chain of literary communication: the subsequent reception of the literary text. The word on the artist's canvas is, we are told, decipherable except for the doubt concerning one letter, a '*d*' or a '*t*.' However, either letter makes perfect sense: 'solitaire' or 'solidaire' (I, 1652) although there is a clear difference of meaning involved. In other words, what we are confronted with is a problem of interpretation. Interpretation involves the deciphering of texts and is part of the act of reading itself, even when all the characters on the page can be made out by the reader without the slightest ambiguity. The present passage merely provides an extreme example of a general process inseparable from the reading of literature. Precisely because of the extreme and exceptional nature of the example it provides, it highlights in what can be seen to be a very self-conscious manner and lays heavy stress upon a process with which the reader has already been necessarily involved from the moment he picked up the book. In other words, this process has not awaited this moment at the conclusion of the short story to come into being but for the first time the reader has been made directly aware of it. In this sense, this last sentence is a *repetition* of all that has gone before, although not within the substance of the preceding text but rather what has gone on in the mind of the reader so far. It reflects the interpretative activity the reader has been involved in. It does therefore stand in relation to the whole of the text as does the microcosm to the macrocosm once one appreciates the fact that what is involved here is not the text-for-itself, so to speak, but the text-for-its-reader. It provides a reflection of the text's perception and reception. Thus, paradoxically, within the text itself, we find, as it were, an anticipation of its own destiny, a reflection of what is to be and yet awaits the coming of the reader. As for the latter, it throws back to him a mirror image of the very activity he is at present engaged in. In other words, we have here what Lucien Dällenbach calls a 'mise-en-abyme de l'énonciation.'[1] But what is even more curious in the present passage is that whereas the *énonciation* we are here considering is on the level of the text's reception, we have already seen in the previous chapter that this selfsame sentence, through the manner in which it also furnishes a reflection of the text's generation, also operates as a *mise-en-abyme* of the text's production. It thereby brings together in a remarkably succinct and yet complex fashion an image of the whole process of *énonciation*. However, it is the reflection of the text's reception or the hermeneutic paradigm that is the concern of this chapter.

The hermeneutic paradigm is also represented in a number of the passages quoted in Chapter 1 where linguistic signs are evoked. The herd of dromedaries in 'La Femme adultère' are seen as 'des signes d'une étrange écriture dont il fallait déchiffrer le sens' (I, 1567), while in 'L'Eté,' the narrator speaks of being able to 'déchiffr[er] l'écriture du monde' (II, 62) through the sensations transmitted through his own skin. The problem of interpretation is also present in the substance of the very fiction of the short story 'L'Hôte,' for when Daru finds his own death sentence written on the blackboard in his classroom: 'Tu as livré notre frère. Tu paieras' (I, 1621), this is precisely the result of a certain interpretation of his own conduct with the Arab prisoner that has been made by the rebels, in this case, as it turns out, a false interpretation. However, if one text more than any other in the Camusian canon features the hermeneutic paradigm, it is surely Camus' first published novel, *L'Etranger*.

The whole history of the exceptionally extensive body of criticism[2] that has been devoted to *L'Etranger* since its appearance in 1942 until the present reveals a continual concern with the problem of how to interpret this novel. Whether it be the exact significance of its title[3] (for whom is Meursault a stranger and from what is he alienated?), the character of its protagonist[4] (is Meursault's conduct the result of

an awareness of the absurdity of existence that has taken place prior
to his mother's death or is he merely an unreflective *bon sauvage* who
comes into conflict with society and its laws, like Lennie in Steinbeck's
Of Mice and Men?), the problem of to whom one should attribute the
book's irony[5] (to the narrator or to his creator?), or the difficulty of
accounting not only for the murder of the Arab on the beach[6] but
more particularly for the four extra shots that the hapless murderer
(whom the reader is led to believe to be more sinned against than
sinning) pumps into the body of his victim after the trigger of his
revolver has initially given way to the instinctive clenching of his
finger as a reaction to the blinding rays of the midday Mediterranean
sun, all of these crucial aspects of the tale have preoccupied and
puzzled the critics. Underlying all these questions is the foremost
problem of the book's narrative technique, since until it has been
resolved, there is little hope of elucidating either character or plot. Is
the tale a kind of diary with a narrative perspective that is shifting
from a temporal point of view, as critics such as M.-G. Barrier[7] and
J.-C. Pariente[8] have maintained, or is it, on the contrary, a kind of
interior monologue recounted after Meursault has heard his death
sentence pronounced as he sits waiting in his death cell, as R.
Champigny[9] and myself[10] have claimed? In fact, one comes to the
conclusion that what is significant with regard to the narrative
perspective[11] is precisely this ambiguity (which I shall return to to
'interpret' after a fashion in the next chapter when I consider the
problem of the text's status as written language or oral discourse), an
ambiguity which, in the final analysis, the text itself does not allow
one to resolve in any wholly satisfactory manner.[12]

What does *not* emerge from the study of the plethora of critical
writings analysing Camus' first novel is any real consideration of the
possibility that the critical enigma that it appears to constitute be itself
an essential attribute of the text that already points to the core of its
specificity. What if the texts of its critics were in fact to be seen as a
direct reflection of the functioning of the text being scrutinized precisely to the extent that the former throws into sharp relief the very
problem of interpretation? Could the wood have been obscured by
the trees?

Before espousing such a critically attractive position with too great
an alacrity, it should first of all be remarked that however one chooses

to view this novel, the problem of interpretation is clearly central to any account of it. This is evident from its opening lines that evoke the problem of interpreting that most succinct of texts, a telegram: 'Aujourd'hui, maman est morte. Ou peut-être hier, je ne sais pas. J'ai reçu un télégramme de l'asile: "Mère décédée. Enterrement demain. Sentiments distingués." CELA NE VEUT RIEN DIRE.' (I, 1125) On the most readily accessible level of the story, it is obvious to each and every reader that we have in the story of the little man as a necessary victim of society a twentieth-century version of the hero of the literature of Romanticism,[13] which lends considerable credence to the view that French literary Existentialism is the descendant of French nineteenth-century mal du siècle, a direct critique of the way in which the legal system wilfully, or at least of necessity, distorts reality to its own ends, thereby indulging in a form of inauthentic interpretation of the lives of its victims that facilitates their condemnation. Moreover, such distortion is by no means the prerogative of the prosecution. When Meursault has his first meeting with his lawyer, the latter points out to him that the authorities had learned that he had 'fait preuve d'insensibilité' on the day of his mother's funeral and apologizes for having to question his client about such a delicate matter in the following terms: '"Vous comprenez, m'a dit mon avocat, cela me gêne un peu de vous demander cela. Mais c'est très important. Et ce sera un gros argument pour l'accusation, si je ne trouve rien à répondre." ... Il m'a demandé si j'avais eu de la peine ce jour-là.' (I, 1170) When Meursault replies: 'Sans doute, j'aimais bien maman, mais cela ne voulait rien dire. Tous les êtres sains avaient plus ou moins souhaité la mort de ceux qu'ils aimaient,' his lawyer's reaction is significantly unambiguous. Not only does he not seek to clarify further such socially unacceptable sentiments even for his own benefit, but he expressly forbids his client to reveal the truth either in court or to the examining magistrate, going beyond proffering his advice in this respect to the point of getting Meursault to explicitly promise to conceal the truth: 'Ici, l'avocat m'a coupé et a paru très agité. Il m'a fait promettre de ne pas dire cela à l'audience, ni chez le magistrat instructeur.' (I, 1170) Not only is the search for the truth in the form of the accused's actual motivation not pursued with any diligence, but the truth is systematically and automatically suppressed once it shows signs of emerging and becoming available for public scrutiny. It must not be allowed to get in the way of the legal fiction that is just as necessary to ensure the effective defence of the accused as it is to procure his conviction. The actual trial thereby becomes and is intended to be a battle between straw men set up and manipulated by the lawyer for the defence and the lawyer for the prosecution. The first gives us 'un honnête homme, un travailleur régulier, infatigable, fidèle à la maison qui l'employait, aimé de tous et compatissant aux misères d'autrui ... un fils modèle qui avait soutenu sa mère aussi longtemps qu'il l'avait pu.' (I, 1197) The second builds up the portrait of someone who 'n'en avai[t] pas, d'âme,' for whom 'rien d'humain, et pas un des principes moraux qui gardent le cœur des hommes [n']était accessible' and who is therefore responsible for the act of patricide a prisoner is due to be tried for the next day in the same court, for 'un homme qui tuait moralement sa mère se retranchait de la société des hommes au même titre que celui qui portait une main meurtrière sur l'auteur de ses jours.' (I, 1195) The 'therefore' is here as weighty as the one Meursault utters to himself in his cell: 'Donc (et le difficile c'était de ne pas perdre de vue tout ce que ce "donc" représentait de raisonnements), donc je devais accepter le rejet de mon pourvoi.' (I, 1204) The point is not that these two portraits cannot *both* be true but rather that neither is, in the final analysis, any more or less false than the other. In spite of his obvious good will and desire to help his lawyer out, Meursault's scrupulousness and honesty prevents him from being able to say with any certainty or conviction any more than that he would have preferred that his mother had not died. Whereupon his lawyer retorts: 'Ceci n'est pas assez.' (I, 1170) What is in fact needed is something more or rather something else: 'Il m'a demandé s'il pouvait dire que ce jour-là j'avais dominé mes sentiments naturels. Je lui ai dit: "Non, parce que c'est faux".' (I, 1170) Their conversation is at cross-purposes, for Meursault has not the slightest inkling that the criterion of truth or falsehood is utterly irrelevant and it is clear that, as his lawyer finally blurts out in exasperation, the accused has 'jamais eu de rapports avec la justice.' (I, 1171) If all the world is a stage, the sphere of legal proceedings of any kind is doubly so. It properly belongs not to the world of fact but to that of fiction, where the operative criterion is not that of truth but of verisimilitude.

All this could not emerge more unambiguously than it does in the second part of *L'Etranger* and I hope it is clear that it is not merely the image of Meursault conjured up, in the full sense of the term, by the prosecution that is involved in the present discussion but rather all the various and indeed conflicting portraits of the protagonist that emerge from the judicial process that wholly occupies the second part of the novel. This is why I have been at some pains to draw out the full implications of the exchange between Meursault and his lawyer. The fact that the latter's activity in conducting his client's defence is as blatantly an exercise in fiction-making or, as the delightfully ambiguous expression has it, character-building, as that of the prosecution whose sole aim is to secure his conviction at any cost is much more significant than the biased distortion the facts of Meursault's life are subjected to by the opposing lawyer.

It is interesting to note in passing how the resulting dramatic situation, reminiscent of a kind of morality tale where Good (Meursault's lawyer) and Evil (the lawyer for the prosecution) dispute the cause of this twentieth-century Everyman (Meursault), is none too subtly undermined by the irony indulged in by the novelist.[14] Whereas Camus seeks, in René Girard's words, to present 'the trial as a parody of justice,'[15] he ends up by giving us the impression that it is not so much 'justice' that is a parody of what it is supposed to be but rather Camus' evocation of it, which is not quite the same thing. However, the effect thus obtained is all that counts here: the initial morality tale incarnated in the judicial set-up is undercut in order to promote a morality tale of quite a different order that the author explicitly articulated in his preface to the American edition of his novel: 'dans notre société, tout homme qui ne pleure pas à l'enterrement de sa mère risque d'être condamné à mort.' (I, 1920) René Girard, in one of the most illuminating essays written on Camus' fiction, was the first to retort indignantly – and rightly so, on the level of the most basic plausibility – in 1964 that nobody could possibly 'believe that the French judicial system is ruthlessly dedicated to the extermination of little bureaucrats addicted to café au lait, Fernandel movies, and casual love affairs with the boss's secretary.'[16]

If the fictive creations that pass for Meursault in the second part of the novel appear, in the first instance, to render the activity of the lawyers wholly analogous to the work of the novelist as he creates his characters according to the laws of a certain plausibility, when they are placed in relation to the life of Meursault as depicted in the first part of the novel their status as interpretations of the latter immediately emerges, thus creating an affinity between the lawyers' rôle and that of the *reader* of novels. So before reducing this portrayal of the legal system solely to its sociological and indeed, within the Algerian colonial situation, political dimensions,[17] it may be as well to take into consideration its more properly literary significance arising from the resemblances noted between the lawyers' occupation and that of the novelist and his reader. The analogy between legal plausibility and novelistic verisimilitude that both stand in exactly the same relationship to fact or reality and that between the creative reconstitution of past events in the courtroom and both the production and the reception of literary fiction suggest that we have here already the potential for self-commentary on the part of the novel in question. Before exploring how this potential is developed in the functioning of the text, we should not overlook the fact that legal writings have traditionally, together with biblical texts and philological analyses, constituted one of the main branches of hermeneutics or the discipline of textual interpretation.

The whole of the second part of *L'Etranger* is thus centred on the problem of interpretation or more precisely that of inaccurate interpretation. All this interpretative activity is occasioned precisely by the events recounted in the first part. In other words, the second part proposes a number of interpretations or reconstitutions of the preceding part. What is important in the present context is that the reader is convinced of the inaccuracy of a given interpretation (that of the examining magistrate, Meursault's lawyer, or the prosecuting counsel, for example) *not* because it departs from any of the other interpretations proposed since all they have in common is their fictive status as *a posteriori* fabrications, but rather because of the heavy irony[18] that pervades all the scenes involving the confrontation between Meursault and the various representatives of the legal system. This irony rules out any misinterpretation by the reader of the way he is to evaluate the portraits of the protagonist that emerge during the trial and its preliminaries. However, as we shall see, this is not the only operative factor in this respect. What I wish to stress for the moment is that nowhere in the second part of the novel is there provided any explicit corrective of these false portraits of Meursault.

The next and vital stage in my argument is constituted by the recognition of the curious and unexpected similarity between the false

Meursault(s) evoked by the lawyers and the person the reader of the first part had begun to see in his mind's eye before his arrest and trial. This similarity is surprising to say the least and its implications are far-reaching. But before examining them, we must first establish the accuracy of such a comparison.

That the prosecuting lawyer's description of Meursault is virtually identical to the considered interpretation of his character by many readers may be a source of surprise for any left-wing intellectual reader, but it is nonetheless true, as can be readily demonstrated by quoting certain critics, not all among the most obtuse. For example, Jean Onimus considers that Meursault 'nous provoque par son inhumanité' and is led to exclaim that if, as Céleste maintains, 'Meursault est un homme, la vie humaine est impossible.'[19] As for Pierre-Henri Simon, the kind of detachment and indifference that Meursault exhibits 'le place hors de la normale.'[20] Charles Moeller, for his part, feels that 'son absence de sens moral est effrayante' and goes so far as to claim that 'il y a du malade chez lui.'[21] In short, the character is seen by such critics as being, at best, a kind of pathological case. In fact, he can even inspire a positive hatred rather than pity, as he does for Pierre Descaves who sees him as 'une sorte de somnambule' who disgusts him: 'Personnage sommaire et somme toute assez odieux, qui ne peut que dégoûter.'[22]

Moreover, these opinions are based, it should be stressed, on a reading of the *whole* of the novel, including its second part, whereas what I am maintaining here is that the reader can well form such an opinion of the protagonist in reading the account of the events preceding the last chapter of the first part. I am not even claiming that there be any inevitability about his forming such an opinion but rather that the opportunity to do so is clearly offered by the text. These distinctions are important.

To understand how the Meursault of the events leading up to the murder can create the impression of being in some way abnormal is not difficult and it would be fastidious and indeed superfluous to go over yet again critical ground[23] that has been covered time and again. It is his apparent indifference that can be interpreted as complete insensitivity that has caused many a reader to react, in the first instance, after a moment of perplexity, with a feeling of revulsion for the protagonist. His indifference, which manifests itself as a kind of automatic reaction in his constant retort 'Cela m'était égal,' covers virtually every aspect of his existence except his corporal contact with the sand, the sea, and the sky of North Africa, or so it seems to the reader. The lack of career motivation he shows when his employer offers him the chance to go to work in Paris (cf. I, 1153-4), a traditional form of promotion in the context of the French community wherever it may be, is no doubt the least surprising. The exchange between Meursault and his mistress Marie, who seeks to determine the precise nature of his feelings for her and his consequent degree of commitment to their relationship is, however, much more disquieting to the reader and becomes more so as their conversation proceeds. Indeed, Marie's conclusion that her lover is 'bizarre' may well seem to be a rather generous evaluation of his attitude!

Le soir, Marie est venue me chercher et m'a demandé si je voulais me marier avec elle. J'ai dit que cela m'était égal et que nous pourrions le faire si elle le voulait. Elle a voulu savoir alors si je l'aimais. J'ai répondu comme je l'avais déjà fait une fois, que cela ne signifiait rien mais que sans doute je ne l'aimais pas. 'Pourquoi m'épouser alors?' a-t-elle dit. Je lui ai expliqué que cela n'avait aucune importance et que si elle le désirait, nous pouvions nous marier. D'ailleurs, c'était elle qui le demandait et moi je me contentais de dire oui. Elle a observé alors que le mariage était une chose grave. J'ai répondu: 'Non.' Elle s'est tue un moment et elle m'a regardé en silence. Puis elle a parlé. Elle voulait simplement savoir si j'aurais accepté la même proposition venant d'une autre femme, à qui je serais attaché de la même façon. J'ai dit: 'Naturellement.' Elle s'est demandé alors si elle m'aimait et moi, je ne pouvais rien savoir sur ce point. Après un autre moment de silence, elle a murmuré que j'étais bizarre, qu'elle m'aimait sans doute à cause de cela mais peut-être un jour je le dégoûterais pour les mêmes raisons. (I, 1154)

Faced with the ambiguity of so many of the protagonist's gestures concerning his mother's death such as his declining the offer to view his mother's body when he arrives at the old people's home (cf. I, 1127) or his decision, after a moment's hesitation, to light up a cigarette as he keeps vigil overnight in the mortuary (cf. I, 1129), the reader can soon jump to the conclusion that this apparent insensitivity also carries over into his relationship with his mother. The fact that a close reading of the text reveals such a conclusion to be mistaken[24] has far less importance in the present context where we are concerned with the reader's *initial* reaction to the first chapters of the novel.

The point is that the text offers the possibility for such an interpretation of Meursault's character because of its very ambiguity. This ambiguity is moreover compounded by the narrative technique, about which so much has been written so often. Suffice it to say that the ambiguity of the events experienced and the behaviour acted out by the young Algerian office worker is as much due to the manner of their telling as to their actual nature. In the final analysis, such a distinction is itself impossible to maintain since the two are inseparable in this first person narrative. What is clear, however, is that Meursault communicates the same sense of detachment in his recounting of his past life as he did in his living of it. So, on this level too, one may well form the opinion that there is something amiss, if not positively abnormal, in the character of the story-teller. Moreover, it is precisely because this disconcerting person is also the story-teller, a task for which he is so obviously ill equipped, that the reader is forced to face up to the antipathy that he can inspire since contrary to the situation of the reader of any third person narrative, here the reader is called upon to espouse Meursault's own perspective on his life[25] in order to even begin to read his narrative in any coherent manner, in other words in a manner that makes sense to him. There is therefore, for the reader, no way of escaping the problem of interpreting the character of the story-teller and leaving the aforementioned ambiguities intact through the reassuring adoption of a kind of aesthetic distance.

Some critics have drawn the logical conclusion from this state of affairs. Thus Philip Thody sees this ambiguity as intentional on the part of the author, contributing to a certain strategy aimed at obliging his reader to *re*read.[26] This would, it should be mentioned in passing, bring his art as a novelist into line with that of Kafka according to Camus' own reading of the German novelist. 'Tout l'art de Kafka,' wrote Camus, 'est d'obliger le lecteur à relire.' (II, 201) Carina Gadourek also views the situation in this light, claiming that Camus was perfectly aware of the different possible reactions of his reader and that he 'n'a rien fait pour déterminer l'attitude'[27] of the latter. This critic ends up by going one decisive stage further when she maintains, and rightly so in my opinion, that Camus actually *sought* to lead his reader astray: 'Le premier chapitre (de la deuxième partie) donne, en guise de "rappel," mais plutôt POUR INDUIRE LE LECTEUR EN ERREUR, ce qui devait être l'interprétation la plus courante de la première partie: l'avocat évoque l'image d'un Meursault insensible.'[28] The reason for such an authorial strategy[29] is obvious enough. If his hero was to be finally considered by the reader as, in Camus' own words, 'le seul christ que nous méritions' (I, 1921), what could be more appropriate than for him to have been initially rejected by the reader just as Christ himself was denied by Peter? As David Madden points out, 'Camus begins by alienating the reader, but in the end, as we join Meursault in the little-ease, the guilty and the "innocent" are reconciled ...'[30] John Cruickshank is of precisely the same opinion when he speaks of Camus' beginning by discouraging the reader's sympathy for his character while finally succeeding in his difficult objective 'of justifying his hero while at the same time encouraging the reader's reprobation.'[31]

We can see therefore that not only does the text of the first part of the novel lend itself to a very negative reaction on the part of the reader, but there exists a substantial consensus of critical opinion to maintain that herein lies one of the keys to any proper appreciation of its over-all functioning. It is moreover clear, I believe, from the foregoing, to return to the point of the present argument, that there is a distinct resemblance between the view of Meursault as an insensitive drifter through life and the portrait etched in rhetorical vitriol by the lawyer for the prosecution.

What the reader of the trial scene is confronted with when the prosecution gives its reading of Meursault's character is basically his own previous instinctive reaction to the protagonist. Yet at the same time the prosecution also gives an account of the actual events leading up to and including the murder which the reader, having experienced the killing of the Arab from within[32] through Meursault's narrative, knows to be, however plausible, wholly untrue. The fact that Meursault actually identifies with this false account for the purposes of his narration of the trial scene only adds to the reader's appreciation of the falsification of the facts that it represents due to the jarring effect this pseudo-identification produces and the irony that arises from the latter:[33]

J'ai trouvé que sa façon de voir les événements ne manquait pas de clarté. Ce qu'il disait était plausible. J'avais écrit la lettre d'accord avec Raymond pour attirer sa maîtresse et la livrer aux mauvais traitements d'un homme 'de moralité douteuse.' J'avais provoqué sur la plage les adversaires de Raymond. Celui-ci avait été blessé. Je lui avais demandé son revolver. J'étais revenu seul pour m'en servir. J'avais abattu l'Arabe comme je le projetais. J'avais attendu. Et 'pour être sûr que la besogne était bien faite,' j'avais tiré encore quatre balles, posément, à coup sûr, d'une façon réfléchie en quelque sorte. (I, 1194)

But I shall return to this passage later from a rather different perspective. That the description of the killing of the Arab represents such a deformation of the actual course of events inevitably casts doubt on the validity of the portrait of the accused's character – irrespective of the irony mentioned earlier. This leads inevitably to the reader's feeling obliged to reconsider his own previous reaction to the character, in other words to re-evaluate his reading of the first part of the novel. With the realization of the grotesqueness of the account given of Meursault and his life comes the disquieting discovery for the reader that he himself, if he had not already condemned Meursault for his apparent insensitivity, had been on the point of doing just that and thereby rejecting 'le seul christ que nous méritons' (I, 1921), in Camus words. This leads to the judgment of the judge, so to speak, for through his own condemnation of the bad faith, hypocrisy, and lack of concern for the truth exhibited by the protagonists of the legal proceedings, the reader finds himself, in fact, uttering his own self-condemnation – not as a judge, of course, but as a reader and interpreter.

The second part of the novel is therefore not only an interpretation – or rather a number of converging interpretations – of the first part, but also a judgment that is, by implication, pronounced upon the reader's own interpretation of that first part. The reader of the second part is confronted by a patently false interpretation that has at the same time nonetheless been the one that had begun to establish itself within his own mind. He is faced therefore not only by a mirror reflection of his own activity as reader of the preceding text but also by an interpretation that bears a striking resemblance to the result of that selfsame activity. It is important to realize that no explicit corrective to this false portrait of Meursault is provided by the text. As a result, it is not a question for him of simply transforming his nascent view of the character according to indications provided. What is required of him is to go back to his initial task as interpreter and reader and to start all over again, his previous efforts having clearly been invalidated. The enigma that is Meursault remains essentially intact. We now have some idea of who he is not, but very little idea of who he really is. All that has been clarified, in fact, by the second part is his creator's favourable attitude towards him.

There exists in the text an image where Meursault is seen looking at himself in his metal plate as he sits in his cell: 'je me suis regardé dans ma gamelle de fer. Il m'a semblé que mon image restait sérieuse alors même que j'essayais de lui sourire.' (I, 1181) This image can be seen as a *mise-en-abyme* of the experience of the reader. Just as there is a discrepancy between the prisoner's smile and the reflection that he sees in his plate, so the reflection of his own interpretation of Meursault's character that the reader is confronted with in the trial scene is nonetheless subject to a definite, if subtle, distortion through its parodic, if not positively caricatural nature. The metal plate thus functions in relation to the protagonist in a manner that is exactly analogous to the functioning of the whole of the text of the second part of the novel in which it is, so to speak, embedded in relation to the reader. What more appropriate image of autorepresentation could there indeed be than that of the mirror? For we are involved here with a process of autorepresentation. However, whereas more commonly in this type of process, the text refers to itself as text, as we have seen in the case of *La Peste*, here it refers to that dialectical relationship that comes into being through the act of reading and that relates the text to its interpreter. It is that relationship that it reproduces within itself and proffers to the reader, whose reading is thus reduced to a narcissistic exercise from which there is no escape within the confines of the text.

It is interesting to note that previously, in the first part of the novel, the reflective functioning of the mirror had been of a more usual kind where what is reflected is reproduced exactly. I am referring to the curious kind of still-life portrait evoked at the end of the second chapter: 'J'ai fermé mes fenêtres et en revenant j'ai vu dans la glace un bout de table où ma lampe à alcool voisinait avec des morceaux de pain.' (I, 1140)[34] It is significant that contrary to the reflection of

Meursault's face in his plate in the second part, here what is reproduced and *re*presented is a part of the fictive universe as such rather than the hermeneutic situation the text is involved in with the reader. It is as though one kind of autorepresentation of a more straightforward kind prepared the emergence of another, far more subtle form of the same phenomenon, each corresponding to the different textual status of the two parts of the novel.

However, even more interesting than this last passage is Meursault's curious reaction to the journalist at the beginning of the trial. Having noticed all the journalists sitting with their pens poised, he is struck by one in particular who is looking at him: 'Dans son visage un peu asymétrique, je ne voyais que ses deux yeux, très clairs, qui m'examinaient attentivement, sans rien exprimer qui fût définissable. Et j'ai eu l'impression bizarre d'être regardé par moi-même.' (I, 1184)[35] Here, as in the evocation of Meursault looking at his own reflection in the plate, there is a question of identity. The difference, however, lies in the fact that the situation has been reversed. Whereas in the passage quoted earlier Meursault was unable to recognize himself in his own reflection to the extent that his image contained no trace of his efforts to smile, in this case he sees himself in the countenance of another. From the lack of expected identification we have moved to an act of identification which is wholly unexpected. If it is tempting to see in this singular scene the equivalent for the novelist of the painter's signature at the bottom of his canvas since who could this reporter be – 'beaucoup plus jeune, habillé en flanelle grise avec une cravate bleue' (I, 1184) – if not the young reporter from *Alger-République*, Albert Camus, who was sent to cover a number of court cases in Algiers? – it is equally possible to see here a further reflection of the hermeneutic situation. Just as the mirror scene in Meursault's cell reproduced the relationship between the reader and the portrait of the accused as it emerged from the trial, in the same way Meursault's identification with the journalist appears to *re*present the way in which the reader can have the impression of seeing himself in the figure of the judge or even in that of the lawyer for the prosecution in a peculiar variant of the traditional refrain: 'There but for the grace of God go I' where the speaker identifies not with the victim but with his persecutor.

The remarkable symmetry of opposites constituted by these two passages of the novel is itself mirrored elsewhere in the novel in the relationship between two other passages which, taken together, furnish a commentary upon the hermeneutic situation not as interpretation or identification with characters as such but as the actual mechanics of the reading process, particularly in the case of the first person novel, and the manner in which the reader appropriates the text.

Let us first of all look at the least remarkable of the two passages in question. It concerns Meursault's reaction to his lawyer's speaking of his client in the first person:

A un moment donné, cependant, je l'ai écouté parce qu'il disait: 'Il est vrai que j'ai tué.' Puis il a continué sur ce ton, disant 'Je' chaque fois qu'il parlait de moi. J'étais très étonné. Je me suis penché vers un gendarme et je lui ai demandé pourquoi. Il m'a dit de me taire et, après un moment, il a ajouté: 'tous les avocats font ça.' Moi, j'ai pensé que c'était m'écarter encore de l'affaire, me réduire à zéro et, en un certain sens, se substituer à moi. (I, 1196-7)

This is, as the gendarme points out, normal courtroom procedure and is not at all disconcerting to the reader, who would not think twice about it. If anything surprises him at all here it is the protagonist's own astonishment. In short, the passage is quickly passed over by the reader, whose only reaction is to simply register the fact that it confirms one's general impression of the character's naïvete or disingenuousness.

The same is, however, far from true of the passage that preceded it only two pages earlier and that throws a different light on this unremarkable and frequent feature of judicial proceedings. The narrator, through the very manner in which he reports the speech of the lawyer for the prosecution, appears, as pointed out earlier, to espouse this alien and hostile viewpoint on his own life and the events leading up to the killing:

J'avais écrit la lettre d'accord avec Raymond pour attirer sa maîtresse et la livrer aux mauvais traitements d'un homme 'de moralité douteuse.' J'avais provoqué sur la plage les adversaires de Raymond. Celui-ci avait été blessé. Je lui avais demandé son revolver. J'étais revenu seul pour m'en servir. J'avais abattu l'Arabe comme je le projetais. J'avais attendu. Et 'pour être sûr que la besogne était bien faite,' j'avais tiré encore quatre balles, posément, à coup sûr, d'une façon réfléchie en quelque sorte. (I, 1194)

What these two passages have in common is a kind of dislocation of the normal relationship between the speaker and what is being said. In the first case, the lawyer, while giving his own account of the life and character of Meursault, presents the latter as though it were Meursault himself speaking. The result is that the speaker is not whom he appears to be. In the second case, Meursault speaks in his own name while articulating the interpretation of his own life formulated by another. Here it is the substance of what is being said that is not what it seems to be. There is a symmetrical opposition between the two situations. The process that is curiously subverted in both cases is that of identification: the manner in which the speaker normally identifies with his own discourse. The lawyer identifies with his client by speaking in his name while failing to espouse his client's perspective on his past life and substituting for the latter his own reconstruction of it. Meursault does precisely the opposite since he continues to speak for himself and yet identifies with a version of the events prior to the murder that is, in fact, wholly alien to him.

Neither of these two diametrically opposed processes would be possible were it not for the particular status of the first person pronoun. The lawyer uses Meursault's 'I' while himself remaining responsible for its predicate, whereas Meursault does not assume the 'I' of another person but only the predicate of the other 'I.' Taken together, these two passages thus point to the essential function of the first person, which is to enable the speaker to assume, that is to take to himself or appropriate, the linguistic system as such. In the words of Emile Benveniste, 'Le langage est ainsi organisé qu'il permet à chaque locuteur de *s'approprier* la langue entière en se désignant comme *je*.'[36] The first and second persons are, as it were, empty forms always available to each and every speaker for his personal appropriation: 'Le langage propose en quelque sorte des formes "vides" que chaque locuteur en exercice de discours s'approprie et qu'il rapporte à sa "personne," définissant en même temps lui-même comme *je* et un partenaire comme *tu*.'[37] In other words, the only reality 'I' or 'you' refers to is a reality of *énonciation* ('réalité de discours') since each 'I' and 'you' has a reference particular to itself. 'I' means the person who is saying 'I': 'Est "ego" qui *dit* "ego".'[38]

That the existence of such a pronominal form facilitates the reading of the first person novel and the appropriation of such a novelistic text by its reader would appear to be self-evident in the light of Benveniste's analysis. It is the autoreferential character of the first person that makes the appropriation of any narrative written in this person so effective and so complete: 'C'est ... un fait à la fois original et fondamental que ces formes "pronominales" ne renvoient pas à la "réalité" ni à des positions "objectives" dans l'espace ou dans le temps, mais à l'énonciation, chaque fois unique, qui les contient, et REFLECHISSENT AINSI LEUR PROPRE EMPLOI.'[39] It is no doubt more problematic to discern a relationship between Benveniste's account of the functioning of the personal pronouns and the reading process itself, the manner in which the reader appropriates any text whatsoever, and yet such a relationship is certainly suggested by the formulation concerning the act of reading given by Georges Poulet in *La Conscience critique*: 'Quand je lis, je pronounce mentalement un JE, et pourtant ce JE que je prononce n'est pas moi-même.'[40]

Be that as it may, if the functioning of the first person pronoun within language itself can be seen to explain the effectiveness of the first person narrative in the novel, then the radical distinction between the person-oriented pronouns of the first and second persons and the 'non-person' pronouns of the third person may well have something to tell us with regard to the difference between a first person and a third person narrative in the novel. The 'non-person' attribute of the third person pronoun is described in these terms by Benveniste: 'Il faut garder à l'esprit que la "3e personne" est la forme du paradigme verbal (ou pronominal) qui ne renvoie *pas* à une personne, parce qu'elle se réfère à un objet placé hors de l'allocution. Mais elle n'existe et ne se caractérise que par opposition à la personne *je* du locuteur qui, l'énonçant, la situe comme "non-personne".'[41] Such a radical distinction must surely have direct repercussions on the whole activity not only of reader *identification* in the novel but also on the nature of the *reading process* involved in the novel narrated in the third person as opposed to that narrated in the first person.

It is customary to speak of the reader's identifying with a given character in a novel in terms of his 'becoming' that character. I should like to suggest that by turning this formulation around one can better grasp the process in question: in other words, 'Emma Bovary is,' indeed, as Flaubert once said, 'me.' And my twisting of Flaubert's meaning here is itself a demonstration of the potential of the 'shifter' (to use the linguist's term), the pronoun 'me.' I do not become Meursault, but Meursault becomes me. All the various fictional characters my novel reading focuses upon become myself for the duration of my reading if only because the only common denominator of all the various reading experiences involved is precisely myself.

This is true in a particular way of all first person narratives because I do not merely adopt the *viewpoint* of the narrator-protagonist *on* what is related but I become the *speaker* of the discourse which ostensibly owes its existence to him. The viewpoint on the fictive reality is itself a kind of empty, self-orientated slot built into the language of the text exactly analogous to those 'formes "vides",' Benveniste talks about, 'que chaque locuteur en exercice de discours s'approprie et ... rapporte à sa "personne" ...'[42] The first person narrative is the device by which the reader is able to espouse and assume an alien speech act, the discourse of another existing in the fictive mode, and to make it his own.

These two passages of L'Etranger that reveal a kind of disjunction between the 'I' and its predicate mirror the very mechanism by which the reader relates to the text of the first person novel in which they figure. They represent what the Russian formalists have termed 'la dénudation du procédé,'[43] the laying bare of the device that enables the reader to take hold of and identify with the discourse of the fictive narrator. In this way, they too furnish a further example of the 'mise-en-abyme de l'énonciation' and constitute a paradigm of the hermeneutic process on the very first level of the reading process itself.

A critic has written that 'Meursault fait le bonheur des critiques'[44] and any account of the criticism devoted to L'Etranger amply confirms as much. Such a remark is, however, not without its irony for the critic's involvement with this work risks developing in a manner that he certainly did not bargain for, if indeed he ever becomes fully aware of the nature of his predicament. This text constitutes a critical conundrum precisely because its real concern is the whole activity of interpretation and the problems it poses, the story of Meursault being but the occasion for the latter. We have seen that the hermeneutic process is not only thematized with a certain insistence right from the initial telegram announcing the death of Meursault's mother to the professional activities of the lawyers, but is also reflected in a number of symmetrically opposed passages whose relationship to one another itself reproduces a mirroring effect although they themselves are not limited to the actual evocation, within the fiction, of mirrors. What is more, this process is broken down, as though prismatically refracted by the text, into its two component parts: the act of reading and that of interpreting. The result is a text wherein the reader reads the story of his own activity. The experience provided by *L'Etranger* is paradoxically that of its own reading.

The Interpreter Interpreted:
La Chute

Although *La Chute* is narrated in the first person, the 'I' of the
narrative voice is by no means the only 'forme vide' or empty slot
that the text provides for the reader. Even the most cursory reading
of this novel or 'récit' reveals the presence of a silent interlocutor, a
paradoxical phenomenon made possible only because the words of
Clamence's companion are never reported directly by him. Clamence
describes the person with whom he is conversing in terms that are
general enough to have a general applicability and yet concrete
enough to turn a shadow into a presence: he has roughly Clamence's
age, 'l'œil renseigné des quadragénaires qui ont à peu près fait le
tour des choses,' he is 'à peu près bien habillé' and has 'les mains
lisses.' (I, 1478) 'Donc, un bourgeois, à peu près! Mais un bourgeois
raffiné!' (I, 1478) Such is the occupant of the shoes into which the
reader is invited to slip. It is the presence of this 'vous' that changes
fundamentally the manner in which the reader most naturally relates
to the 'I' of a first person narrative. Moreover, the fact that the addressee of the 'I' who is normally none other than the reader himself, that
is to say, more precisely, the 'implied reader'[1] (to use Wolfgang Iser's
term), is incorporated explicitly into the text itself already suggests
that this text may well reflect within its own structure certain aspects
of the hermeneutic process.

However, before pursuing such a line of inquiry, it should first of
all be noted that the activity of interpretation plays a rôle that is
almost as obvious in this later text as it was in *L'Etranger*.

Clamence, the narrator, begins by recounting his past life in considerable detail. Previous to his arrival in Amsterdam, he had been a
successful Parisian lawyer:

J'étais vraiment irreprochable dans ma vie professionnelle. Je n'ai jamais accepté de pot-de-vin, cela va sans dire, mais je ne me suis jamais abaissé non plus à aucune démarche. Chose plus rare, je n'ai jamais consenti à flatter aucun journaliste, pour me le rendre favorable, ni aucun fonctionnaire dont l'amitié pût être utile. (I, 1483)

Hence his feeling of satisfaction at having been so successful in his profession without having compromised himself in any way. Not the least of his satisfaction came from his rôle of defender of the weak and the oppressed:

Ma situation était plus enviable. Non seulement je ne risquais pas de rejoindre le camp des criminels ... mais encore je prenais leur défense, à la seule condition qu'ils fussent de bons meurtriers, comme d'autres sont de bons sauvages. La manière dont je menais cette défense me donnait de grandes satisfactions. (I, 1483)

The alacrity with which he would help blind people or give people directions in the street and his delight at giving money to beggars and worthy causes were indicative of the same penchant in his character. In short, his courtesy and generosity knew no bounds (cf. I, 1484-5). His social success was no less than the acclaim he received from his professional colleagues: 'Familier quand il le fallait, silencieux si nécessaire, capable de désinvolture autant que de gravité, j'étais de plain-pied. Aussi ma popularité était-elle grande et je ne comptais plus mes succès dans le monde.' (I, 1487) His sexuality was assumed by him no less happily: 'la chair, la matière, le physique en un mot qui déconcerte ou décourage tant d'hommes dans l'amour ou dans la solitude, m'apportait, sans m'asservir, des joies égales. J'étais fait pour avoir un corps.' (I, 1488) In other words, his existence was, from beginning to end, one long success story the equal of which could hardly be imagined:

N'était-ce pas cela, en effet, l'Eden, cher Monsieur: la vie en prise directe? Ce fut la mienne. Je n'ai jamais eu besoin d'apprendre à vivre. Sur ce point, je savais déjà tout en naissant. Il y a des gens dont le problème est de s'abriter des hommes, ou du moins de s'arranger d'eux. Pour moi, l'arrangement était fait ... Je n'étais pas mal fait de ma personne, je me montrais à la fois danseur infatigable et discret érudit, j'arrivais à aimer en même temps, ce qui n'est guère facile, les femmes et la justice, je pratiquais les sports et les beaux-arts, bref, je m'arrête, pour que vous ne me soupçonniez pas de complaisance. Mais imaginez, je vous prie, un homme dans la force de l'âge, de parfaite santé, généreusement doué, habile dans les exercices du corps comme dans ceux de l'intelligence, ni pauvre ni riche, dormant bien, et profondément content de lui-même sans le montrer autrement que par une sociabilité heureuse. Vous admettrez alors que je puisse parler, en toute modestie, d'une vie réussie. (I, 1487)

The transformation that eventually comes about in his view of his own existence can well be illustrated by contrasting his early description of it as 'la vie en prise directe' with his later experience as he looks into his bathroom mirror: 'Mon image souriait dans la glace, mais il m'a semblé que mon sourire était double ...' (I, 1493) In fact, his relationship to his Parisian existence had been too spontaneous and unreflective for one to be able to speak of his having had a 'view' of it: 'Oui, peu d'êtres ont été plus naturels que moi. Mon accord avec la vie était total, j'adhérais à ce qu'elle était, du haut en bas ...' (I, 1481)

What happens subsequently is that certain events oblige him to take stock of his life and to scrutinize it for the first time. The events in question are, first of all, the sudden awareness one day of somebody laughing behind his back without his being able to determine any precise source of the laughter (cf. I, 1493) and, secondly, his failure to go to the aid of a young woman who commits suicide by jumping off a bridge into the river Seine (cf. I, 1509). The results of this scrutiny constitute a complete interpretation of his past life as he had previously recounted it to his listener.

The first example he gives illustrates this very well. Earlier he had sketched the scene of his coming to the aid of a blind man in the street:

Du plus loin que j'apercevais une canne hésiter sur l'angle d'un trottoir, je me précipitais, devançais d'une seconde, parfois, la main charitable qui se tendait déjà, enlevais l'aveugle à toute autre sollicitude que la mienne et le menais d'une main douce et ferme sur le passage clouté, parmi les obstacles de la circulation, vers le havre tranquille du trottoir où nous nous séparions avec une émotion mutuelle. (I, 1484)

He now gives a quite different interpretation of the same action:

Tenez, peu de temps après le soir dont je vous ai parlé, j'ai découvert quelque chose. Quand je quittais un aveugle sur le trottoir où je l'avais aidé à atterrir, je le saluais. Ce coup de chapeau ne lui était évidemment pas destiné, il ne pouvait pas le voir. A qui donc s'adressait-il? Au public. Après le rôle, les saluts. Pas mal, hein? (I, 1498)

His fine motivation in devoting his professional existence to the defence of widows, orphans, and 'bons meurtriers' (I, 1483) – the name of Meursault comes to mind under the latter category and not without reason! – is also subject to a wholly different and far less praiseworthy interpretation:

J'apprenais du moins que je n'étais du côté des coupables, des accusés, que dans la mesure exacte où leur faute ne me causait aucun dommage. Leur culpabilité me rendait éloquent parce que je n'en étais pas la victime. Quand j'étais menacé, je ne devenais pas seulement un juge à mon tour, mais plus encore: un maître irascible qui voulait, hors de toute loi, assommer le délinquant et le mettre à genoux. Après cela, mon cher compatriote, il est bien difficile de continuer sérieusement à se croire une vocation de justice et le défenseur prédestiné de la veuve et de l'orphelin. (I, 1502)

The episode of his altercation with the motorcyclist at the traffic lights which ends with his being struck by an onlooker and being called a 'pauvre type' (cf. I, 1499-51), when he recalls it to mind, gives rise to the following unflattering interpretation:

Eh bien, quand je retrouvai le souvenir de cette aventure, je compris ce qu'elle signifiait. En somme mon rêve n'avait pas résisté à l'épreuve des faits. J'avais rêvé, cela était clair maintenant, d'être un homme complet, qui se serait fait respecter dans sa personne comme dans son métier. Moitié Cerdan, moitié de Gaulle, si vous voulez. Bref, je voulais dominer en toutes choses. C'est pourquoi je prenais des airs, je mettais mes coquetteries à montrer mon habileté physique plutôt que mes dons intellectuels. Mais, après avoir été frappé en public sans réagir, il ne m'était plus possible de caresser cette belle image de moi-même. Si j'avais été l'ami de la vérité et de l'intelligence que je prétendais être, que m'eût fait cette aventure déjà oubliée de ceux qui en avaient été les spectateurs? A peine me serais-je accusé de m'être fâché pour rien, et aussi, étant fâché, de n'avoir pas su faire face aux conséquences de ma colère, faute de présence d'esprit. Au lieu de cela, je brûlais de prendre ma revanche, de frapper et de vaincre. Comme si mon véritable désir n'était pas d'être la créature la plus intelligente ou la plus généreuse de la terre, mais seulement de battre qui je voudrais, d'être le plus fort enfin, et de la façon la plus élémentaire. (I, 1501-2)

What Clamence now gives his listener is a complete and self-devastating interpretation of the life he had previously recounted in such glowing terms. Nothing of the previous portrait is allowed to remain intact:

Il faut le reconnaître humblement, mon cher compatriote, j'ai toujours crevé de vanité. Moi, moi, moi, voilà le refrain de ma chère vie, et qui s'entendait dans tout ce que je disais ... Quand je m'occupais d'autrui, c'était pure condéscendance, en toute liberté, et le mérite me revenait, je montais d'un degré dans l'amour que je me portais.

Avec quelques autres vérités, j'ai découvert ces évidences peu à peu, dans la période qui suivit le soir dont je vous ai parlé. (I, 1498)

It would be fastidious and no doubt superfluous to quote all these revisions of the earlier portrait, such as his analysis of his relations with the other sex (cf. I, 1507-8). I have, I believe, made my point that having given a detailed account of his past life as a Parisian lawyer, the narrator then proceeds to give an interpretation or, at least, a *re*interpretation of his existence before he exchanged the banks of the Seine for the canals of Amsterdam. This second part of his narrative (beginning on page 1498) therefore stands in relation to the pages preceding it very much as the second part of *L'Etranger* stands in relation to the first part: it provides an interpretation of what has already been recounted.

The reader has no reason to cast doubt on the validity of Clamence's unfavourable interpretation of his past life. On the contrary, since the narrator does everything in his power to engage the complicity of his listener, constantly seeking his agreement: 'Chaque homme a besoin d'esclaves comme d'air pur. Commander, c'est respirer, VOUS ETES BIEN DE CET AVIS? ... Par exemple, VOUS AVEZ DU LE REMARQUER, notre

vieille Europe philosophe enfin de la bonne façon.' (I, 1496) Even to
the point of flattering him shamelessly: 'Enfin, je vous amuse, ce qui,
sans vanité, suppose chez vous une certaine ouverture d'esprit' (I,
1478), appealing both to his intelligence and to his sensitivity: 'Ici,
nous sommes dans le dernier cercle. Le cercle des ... Ah! Vous savez
cela? Diable, vous devenez difficile à classer. Mais vous comprenez
alors pourquoi je puis dire que le centre des choses est ici, bien que nous
nous trouvions à l'extrémité du continent. UN HOMME SENSIBLE
COMPREND CES BIZARRERIES.' (I, 1481) In spite of the cynical tone of his
tale, he does in fact go so far as to solicit explicitly his listener's
sympathy:

*Mais permettez-moi de faire appel à notre ami le primate. Hochez la tête pour
le remercier et, surtout, buvez avec moi, j'ai besoin de votre sympathie.*

*Je vois que cette déclaration vous étonne. N'avez-vous jamais eu subitement
besoin de sympathie, de secours, d'amitié. Oui, bien sûr.* (I, 1489)

Moreover, much of the substance of his narrative is of such a general
nature that it consists of what amounts to a series of maxims:[2]

*Je rêve parfois de ce que diront de nous les historiens futurs. Une phrase leur
suffira pour l'homme moderne: il forniquait et lisait les journaux.* (I, 1477)

Quand on n'a pas de caractère, il faut bien se donner une méthode. (I, 1479)

*L'homme est ainsi, cher Monsieur, il a deux faces: il ne peut pas aimer sans
s'aimer.* (I, 1490)

*Nul homme n'est hypocrite dans ses plaisirs, ai-je lu cela ou l'ai-je pensé, mon
cher compatriote?* (I, 1507)

One has little difficulty in subscribing to a general 'truth' of this kind,
for one is hardly committing oneself in any precise sense of the term
by so doing. The function of the innumerable maxims that punctuate
Clamence's narrative is thus to gain the reader/listener's confidence
and to create a sense of complicity in the latter: 'Je n'ai plus d'amis, je
n'ai que des complices. En revanche, leur nombre a augmenté, ils
sont le genre humain. Et dans le genre humain, vous le premier.' (I,
1511)

The reader therefore goes along with Clamence's unflattering interpretation of his past life as a successful lawyer and even finds himself empathizing with the narrator in the exercise of his newfound lucidity which, in spite of the cynicism it appears to have given rise to, is not without a positive therapeutic moral value. However, to identify with such a *mea culpa* is inevitably to end up applying the same hypercritical judgments to one's own existence. Such is precisely the end that Clamence has in mind. Having pointed out that hell must be where each house bears a shopkeeper's sign indicating its owner's character, 'Dupont, philosophe froussard, ou propriétaire chrétien, ou humaniste adultère' (I, 1497) and where each of us finds himself classified once and for all, Clamence adds significantly: 'Vous, par exemple, mon cher compatriote, pensez un peu à ce que serait votre enseigne. Vous vous taisez? Allons, vous me répondrez plus tard.' (I, 1497) After recounting a particularly obnoxious episode involving one of his mistresses, he acquiesces in the negative judgment he anticipates in his listener but not without formulating an immediate riposte: 'Je conviendrai avec vous malgré votre courtois silence, que cette aventure n'est pas très reluisante. Songez pourtant à votre vie, mon cher compatriote! Creusez votre mémoire, peut-être y trouverez-vous quelque histoire semblable que vous me conterez plus tard.' (I, 1506-7) Thus, in psychological terms, the confession becomes at the same time an accusation and a putting-in-question of the addressee.

However, on the level of the text as such and its relationship to the reader in the act of reading, there are other consequences. Having accepted a certain interpretation of the conduct and character of a fictive personage named Jean-Baptiste Clamence, the reader finds himself being pressed to apply this selfsame interpretation, or at least an analogous one, to his own life. What is being called upon here is not the reader's normal potential as a reader – his imagination and his ability to recreate and identify with lives conjured up by the novelist – but his moral qualities as a human being. Fiction and fact are becoming inextricably intertwined in a most disconcerting manner. The hypothetical reader who is built into the text in the form of Clamence's unheard companion gives way to the person actually reading the novel. The addressee is no longer the fictive person programmed into the text, so to speak, but a real person, whoever happens to pick up the book. Instead of being asked in the normal expected fashion to interpret a work of literature, the latter is forced into an exercise in moral self-scrutiny.

If, in psychological terms, one could rightly speak of the reader's having fallen into a trap, in terms of the functioning of the text we have a far more interesting situation. The model that the text proposes is none other than that of the appropriation of the literary text. The hermeneutic practice of texts involves the self-discovery of the reader. To interrogate a text is, in the final analysis, to interrogate oneself. Paul Ricœur describes the process involved in these terms:

Hermeneutics and reflective philosophy are here correlative and reciprocal: on the one hand, self-understanding provided a round-about way of understanding of the cultural signs in which the self contemplates himself and forms himself; on the other hand, the understanding of a text is not an end in itself and for itself; it mediates the relation to himself of a subject who, in the short circuit of immediate reflefction, would not find the meaning of his own life ... In short, in hermeneutical reflection − or in reflective hermeneutics − the constitution of self *and that of meaning are contemporaneous.*[3]

The dialogue with the text is necessarily accompanied by the progressive discovery of self since this dialogue consists of a reciprocal interrogation: just as I interrogate the work, 'l'œuvre m'interroge,' in its turn, as Jean Starobinski remarks, and 'je me sens *exposé* à cette question qui vient à ma rencontre.'[4]

We have seen that this text appeals very directly and very clearly to the existential experience of its reader, demanding of the latter that he implicate himself. In this respect, it militates in favour of the conditions necessary for the understanding of any text and thus activates the process of reading-understanding-interpreting. As Hans-Georg Gadamer explains, 'All that is asked is that we remain open to the meaning of the other person or of the text. But this openness always includes our placing the other meaning in a relation with the whole of our own meanings or ourselves in a relation to it.'[5] Clamence insists, as we have seen, that the other person apply the tale he has told to himself: 'pensez un peu à ce qui serait votre enseigne.' (I, 1497) Given his interlocutor's silence, the only other person left to apply it to himself is the reader: 'Songez pourtant à votre vie, mon cher compatriote!' (I, 1506) Now, it should be noted that in the same way that 'interpretation is not an occasional additional act of understanding, but rather understanding is always an interpretation,' 'understanding always involves something like the application of a text to be understood to the present situation of the interpreter.'[6] In other words, the reader of *La Chute* finds himself obliged to fulfil the very conditions necessary for the understanding of a text. To quote Gadamer once again, 'In order to understand [the text], he must not seek to disregard himself and his particular hermeneutical situation. He must relate the text to this situation, if he wants to understand it at all.'[7] It is just such a relationship that comes necessarily and automatically into being in this text of Camus' which, through its very structure, already maps out the form and procedures of the hermeneutic process.

This is, however, not the end of the process which the functioning of this text brings into play. The proferred interpretation of Clamence's earlier existence is not allowed to co-exist for very long with the reader's self-scrutiny. The former is finally revealed for the fiction that it has always necessarily been, except that in the present case the fiction is doubly fictive, a fiction within a fiction. Moreover, intimations of its fictivity accompanied its elaboration from the very beginning:

La face de toutes mes vertus avait ainsi un revers moins imposant. Il est vrai que, dans un autre sens, mes défauts tournaient à mon avantage. L'obligation où je me trouvais de cacher la partie vicieuse de ma vie me donnait par exemple un air froid que l'on confondait avec celui de la vertu, mon indifférence me valait d'être aimé, mon égoïsme culminait dans mes générosités. JE M'ARRETE: TROP DE SYMETRIE NUIRAIT A MA DEMONSTRATION. (I, 1517)

Does the narrator not warn us to beware of any kind of apparent confession? 'je n'aime plus que les confessions, et les auteurs de confession écrivent surtout pour ne pas se confesser, pour ne rien dire de ce qu'ils savent. Quand ils passent aux aveux, c'est le moment de se méfier ...' (I, 1536) The truth of the substance of his narrative is, in fact, explicitly put in question: 'Je sais ce que vous pensez: il est bien difficile de démêler le vrai du faux dans ce que je raconte. Je confesse que vous avez raison.' (I, 1535) The implication is clear enough:

'Qu'importe après tout? Les mensonges ne mettent-ils pas finalement sur la voie de la vérité? Et mes histoires, vraies ou fausses, ne tendent-elles pas toutes à la même fin, n'ont-elles pas le même sens?' (ɪ, 1535) Inventiveness with a certain aim in view has played a greater part in the whole of Clamence's narrative than any concern for the truth. Had he not spoken much earlier of his 'digressions' and of 'les efforts d'une invention à laquelle, je l'espère, vous rendez justice'? (ɪ, 1508)

Not only is the narrator's interpretation of his past life finally revealed to be at the very least wholly unreliable and more likely a pure fabrication from beginning to end but so too is the earlier account of the very facts of his previous existence. The interpretation the reader had subscribed to having disappeared into thin air together with the very object of that interpretation, Clamence's life in Paris, the reader has nothing left to interpret other than his own existence.

Just as the text had, in the first place, provided its own interpretation of itself in the form of Clamence's evaluation of his own past conduct, so the text now provides its own explicit commentary on the functioning of its narrative:

Je m'accuse, en long et en large. Ce n'est pas difficile, j'ai maintenant de la mémoire. Mais attention, je ne m'accuse pas grossièrement, à grands coups sur la poitrine. Non, je navigue souplement, je multiplie les nuances, les digressions aussi, j'adapte enfin mon discours à l'auditeur, j'amène ce dernier à renchérir. Je mêle ce qui me concerne et ce qui regarde les autres. Je prends les traits communs, les expériences que nous avons ensemble souffertes, les faiblesses que nous partageons, le bon ton, l'homme du jour enfin, tel qu'il sévit en moi et chez les autres. Avec cela, je fabrique un portrait qui est celui de tous et de personne. Un masque en somme, assez semblable à ceux du carnaval, à la fois fidèles et simplifiés, et devant lesquels on se dit: 'Tiens, je l'ai rencontré, celui-là.' Quand le portrait est terminé, comme ce soir, je le montre, plein de désolation: 'Voilà, hélas! ce que je suis.' Le réquisitoire est achevé. Mais, du même coup, le portrait que je tends à mes contemporains devient un miroir. (ɪ, 1545)

Thus the necessary complicity has been nurtured for the reader, who had thought to console Clamence with his sympathy and understanding, to find himself finally alone in the prisoner's dock:

Couvert de cendres, m'arrachant lentement les cheveux, le visage labouré par les ongles, mais le regard perçant, je me tiens devant l'humanité entière, récapitulant mes hontes, sans perdre de vue l'effet que je produis, et disant: 'J'étais le dernier des derniers.' Alors, insensiblement, je passe, dans mon discours, du 'je' au 'nous.' Quand j'arrive au 'voilà ce que nous sommes,' le tour est joué, je peux dire leurs vérités. Je suis comme eux, bien sûr, nous sommes dans le même bouillon. J'ai cependant une supériorité, celle de le savoir, qui me donne le droit de parler ... Plus je m'accuse et plus j'ai le droit de vous juger. Mieux, je vous provoque à vous juger vous-même, ce qui me soulage d'autant. Ah! mon cher, nous sommes d'étranges, de misérables créatures et, pour peu que nous revenions sur nos vies, les occasions ne manquent pas de nous étonner et de nous scandaliser nous-même. Essayez. J'écouterai, soyez-en sûr, votre propre confession, avec un grand sentiment de fraternité. (I, 1545-6)

As in the case of *L'Etranger*, there is a parallel to be drawn here between the theme of judgment and the act of interpretation. Clamence has an aversion for judges which he clearly shares with the author of *L'Etranger*: 'j'étais soutenu par des sentiments sincères: la satisfaction de me trouver du bon côté de la barre et un mépris instinctif envers les juges en général ... je ne pouvais comprendre qu'un homme se désignât lui-même pour cette surprenante fonction.' (I, 1482) He has no greater desire than that of avoiding being judged himself: 'il s'agit ... de couper au jugement, d'éviter d'être toujours jugé, sans que jamais la sentence soit prononcée.' (I, 1512) His narrative has no other aim: '[Mon discours] est orienté par l'idée ... d'éviter personnellement le jugement ... Le grand empêchement à y échapper n'est-il pas que nous sommes les premiers à nous condamner? Il faut donc commencer par étendre la condamnation à tous, sans discrimination, afin de la délayer déjà.' (I, 1541) And he has finally hit upon the means to attain this end: 'Puisqu'on ne pouvait condamner les autres sans aussitôt se juger, il fallait s'accabler soi-même pour avoir le droit de juger les autres. Puisque tout juge finit un jour en pénitent, il fallait prendre la route en sens inverse et faire métier de pénitent pour pouvoir finir en juge.' (I, 1544) Just as Clamence thereby escapes the judgment of others and is able to end up the judge rather than the judged, so the text through the singular and formally unorthodox manner of its functioning manages to frustrate all attempts on the part of its reader to interpret it. The latter is no more in a position to interpret this curiously open-ended text than he is to judge the loquacious and elusive spinner of tales he has been listening to.

For when the whole substance of Clamence's narrative collapses before the reader's very eyes, so to speak, leaving the interpreter to his own devices – such as a *mea culpa* to be enunciated on his own behalf – there remains the accusing finger of his judge and, indeed, the judge himself. The presence of the story-teller is all that survives the destructive effect of the final revelation of the point of his narrative. But survive it certainly does, since from the very beginning of the text, the reality of the Amsterdam bar and the concentric circles of the canals of the Dutch capital are established for the reader beyond any shadow of doubt, as is the bedroom in which Clamence receives his interlocutor for the last time. In fact, the greater part of the novel consists of *two* novelistic universes rather than one that appear to be separated only by time and space: that of Amsterdam where the tale is being told and that of Paris where Clamence had practised as a lawyer. It is only subsequently, as we have seen, that it is revealed that what really distinguishes them is all that separates fact from fantasy. What remains then when the narrator's ingenious house of cards is allowed to collapse is the story-teller himself. This is necessarily so since his presence is interdependent with the *case vide* provided by the 'vous,' his unheard companion. Once the possibility of his having lied from the beginning of his encounter with the stranger in the bar and having had no other objective than to ensnare the latter into making his own 'confession' is entertained, then the figure of the self-styled 'juge-pénitent' becomes a completely unknown quantity. Elsewhere, I have compared the presence we are left with at the end of *La Chute* to that of the actor on the stage after the final curtain has fallen.[8] The rôle of a certain 'Jean-Baptiste Clamence' has been played out by the one-time make-believe pope and at the end of the performance, as he prepares to take off his make-up and costume, the actor removes his mask, 'un masque en somme, assez semblable à ceux du carnaval.' (I, 1545) It is this unknown person, this complete stranger who is pointing an accusing finger at myself as I close the book.

The image taken from the theatre is indeed singularly appropriate. Perhaps only in the theatre do we experience fact and fiction, reality and make-believe, as contiguous spaces in a state of material co-existence, the footlights constituting the line of demarcation between the two, between those living out a fiction and those witnessing it. Such too is precisely the case of the present text. The real-life reader (as opposed to any 'implied reader') is confronted by and feels, if not threatened, condemned by a fictive creature. In the mirror which the latter holds out for me as I read this tale, to contemplate myself in, there is a curious coming together and intermingling of the human reality that I am and the world of fiction. When reference was made earlier to the account of Clamence's past life and his interpretation of it finally revealing itself for the fiction it was, I should rather have spoken of their status as being doubly fictive: a fiction *within* a fiction. It is by the very particular way that I the reader am engaged by this text that its specificity can best be defined. Having been drawn into the world of the fiction of the Amsterdam bar by dutifully occupying the empty slot provided for me, I find that it was not as a reader that my services were required, but as a human being prepared to put into question and scrutinize his own existence outside the world of tales and their tellers. (Such an objective, it should be added, was, as we have seen, far from foreign to the author of *L'Etranger*.) Once I was comfortably ensconced within this novelistic world of make-believe, its fictive attributes gradually fell away in a subtle process of steady erosion until I found myself living 'for real,' so to speak, the 'malconfort' which I thought to be the situation of the story-teller.

Thus the uneasy co-existence of two contiguous worlds that tend to merge with one another while, at the same time, being fundamentally incompatible with one another is, in my view, the feature of this text that, better than any other, can be said to characterize its specificity. (Here I refer not to the world of the canals of Amsterdam in relation to that of the Paris courts, to the present as compared to the past, but to the bar Mexico-City in which the reader takes his seat to have a drink with a certain Clamence.) This co-existence that brings together fact and fiction and brings about their (con)fusion recalls the 'fusion of horizons' (*Horizontverschmelzung*) as defined by Gadamer, whereby the reader's horizon encounters the text's horizon and progressively assimilates the latter so as to bring into existence a new horizon.

The 'horizon' is defined by the German hermeneuticist as being constituted by the prejudices of the reader which determine the hermeneutical situation and 'constitute, then, the horizon of a particular present, for they represent that beyond which it is impossible to see.'[9] The horizon of the present is in a continual process of formation and cannot be formed without the past. This gives rise to 'the experience of the tension between the text and the present.'[10] Gadamer stresses that 'the hermeneutic task consists in not covering up this tension by attempting a naïve assimilation but consciously bringing it out.'[11] Camus' text indeed brings out and displays this tension for all to see by revealing its structure, the cogs of the mechanism in question, that explicitly determine the manner of its functioning as a text.

The process of the fusion of horizons that is decomposed, displaced, and represented by the text corresponds to the model of conversation. Gadamer introduces this analogy in the following terms:

one is understanding the text itself. But this means that the interpreter's own thoughts have also gone into the re-awakening of the meaning of the text. In this the interpreter's own horizon is decisive, yet not as a personal standpoint that one holds on to or enforces, but more as a meaning and a possibility that one brings into play and puts at risk, and that helps one truly to make one's own what is said in the text. I have described this above as a 'fusion of horizons.' We can now see that this is the full realisation of conversation, in which something is expressed that is not only mine or my author's, but common.[12]

We are now perhaps better able to appreciate the importance and significance of the dialogical form of *La Chute* for the present hermeneutical perspective.

The way in which Clamence's interpretation of his past life proves to be utterly unreliable from beginning to end produces a situation that recalls that which confronts the reader of the second part of *L'Etranger*, who is faced with several false interpretations of Meursault's character and the events leading up to the murder on the beach without the text's offering him any corrective of the latter. The reader of Camus' last novel also finds himself obliged to return to the job of interpreting anew the narrator-protagonist and his character. We have seen that if the reader is finally reduced to scrutinizing his own life, this is because this is all there is left for him to scrutinize as soon as he learns Clamence's real purpose in pretending to confide in him and the real Clamence becomes once again a complete stranger to him. Thus although Clamence's false interpretation of his past existence remains or again becomes operative with the reader's substituting his own life for that of the protagonist as the object of interpretation, the reader does not, for all that, escape the problem of attempting to resolve the enigma that Clamence has become for him, an enigma that cannot but preoccupy him given our natural desire to know the identity of the one who is judging us. In this context, it is important to give due weight to each of the terms 'portrait' and 'miroir' that Clamence employs in his remark: 'Mais, du même coup, le portrait que je tends à mes contemporains devient un miroir.' (I, 1545) The 'portrait' created by Clamence's account of his life is going to enable the reader to recognize himself in it thanks to the traits it shares with his own character and life. But we must not lose sight of the fact that his tale also functions in a completely different fashion with the disappearance of the portrait of a certain Jean-Baptiste Clamence that has turned out to be a complete fabrication: the mirror-portrait has become a mirror and nothing but a mirror. What the reader sees in this mirror is the reflection of his own activity as a reader and an interpreter. Thus it is that the process of autorepresentation is set in motion as it were; but in such a way that it takes in the hermeneutic activity and operates therefore not on the level of the text-for-itself but on that of the text-for-the-reader. In short, to discover that the interpretation Clamence gives of himself is false is, for the reader, to find himself back where he started from as far as interpreting the character and his story is concerned. The text forces the reader to renew his efforts as an interpreter without providing him with the means to do so. The latter is thrown back upon himself and condemned to going round in circles as he watches himself interpreting while having nothing other than himself to interpret.

The revelation at the end of the book is, it goes without saying, unexpected. It represents a complete turnabout on the part of the protagonist-narrator who, in one fell swoop, has turned the tables on the reader. The judge-penitent has become the judge only too ready to pronounce judgment on the reader who, for his part, having identified to a certain extent with the judge-penitent, finds himself reduced to the rôle of penitent. The reader's expectations have not been merely frustrated: they have proved to have been completely unfounded. Every certainty he had thought to have acquired during the course of his reading has collapsed. He had let himself be taken in by appearances that have turned out to be misleading to the point of concealing the very opposite to what they suggested.

The way in which the text ends up by thwarting the reader's expectations by putting in question, or rather contradicting and wiping out, his whole experience of the work up to that point is a major factor in its efficacy in representing, through its very structure, the paradigm of the fusion of horizons evoked earlier. The thwarting of the reader's expectations, a device that has been fully explored by Wolfgang Iser in *The Implied Reader* and *The Act of Reading*,[13] is, in my view, a kind of equivalent, on this level of the reception of the novelistic text, of negative experience in general. According to Gadamer's hermeneutic theory, the fusion of horizons characterizes not only the experience of texts but all types of experience. The phenomenon of experience is 'an essentially negative one' whereby 'continually false generalisations [are] refuted by experience and what was regarded as typical [is] shown not to be so':

If we have an experience of an object, this means that we have not seen the thing correctly hitherto and now know it better. Thus the negativity of experience has a curiously productive meaning. It is not simply a deception that we see through and hence make a correction, but a comprehensive knowledge that we acquire.[14]

It is not, for the reader of *La Chute* either, a question of simply making a 'correction' in the light of a 'deception' created by the false portrait of its protagonist. Rather is it a question of becoming fully aware of what it means to interpret a text and even to read, not to mention the coming to terms with the affinities that exist between the interpreter and the judge.

Let us come back now to the dialogical form of this text. I referred above to Gadamer's conception of the fusion of horizons involved in the understanding of any text as 'the full realisation of conversation.'[15] 'Interpretation, like conversation,' writes Gadamer, 'is a closed circle within the dialectic of question and answer.'[16] One could well be tempted to see the dialogical form of Camus' last novel as anticipating the fate that awaits it and that will come to pass through the activity

of the reader and interpreter. Or even, rather than as a kind of reproduction of that activity that represents the consummation of the literary work, a first movement made by the text towards the fusion of
horizons that is thereby set in motion. The curious structure of this
text whose dialogue tends to encompass and implicate its reader in its
own activity can only encourage such an hypothesis. However, the
textual functioning that characterizes *La Chute* is not quite so simple.

It will come as no surprise to anyone when I point out that,
although this text takes on the appearance of a dialogue, it is nevertheless nothing of the kind. To start with, even though Clamence's
interlocutor does not stay silent, his words are never transcribed as
such. (We must not, however, lose sight of the fact that it is precisely
this aspect of the text that facilitates the fusion of the horizon of the
text with that of the reader through encouraging the latter to slip into
the shoes of Clamence's companion.) What this means is that, while
the fiction stages a *dialogue*, situated between the mists of Amsterdam
and the neon lighting of the bar Mexico-City, the text takes on the
form of a *monologue* given the merely implicit presence of the addressee. Moreover, even on the level of the fictive universe, Clamence
shows a marked tendency to monopolize the conversation, following
in this respect the lead given by modern societies as he sees them:
'Nous avons remplacé le dialogue par le communiqué' (I, 1496-7),
he explains.

In short, the dialogue is an abortive one on the formal level of the
text while constituting, on the level of the fiction of the Amsterdam
bar, a veritable parody of itself. Whether one considers *La Chute* to be
a monologue masquerading as a dialogue or a dialogue reduced to a
monologue by the loquacious Clamence, the result is the same: in the
final analysis, this text merely *mimes* dialogue, going through the
motions of dialogue without ever becoming one.

Notwithstanding this, its form which we can now characterize
more precisely as being potentially or implicitly dialogical in nature,
has the effect of attenuating one of the basic factors at work in any
written text. It is this factor that makes the practice of hermeneutics
necessary. This is the fact that written language is detached both from
its author and from its addressee. 'Writing is central to the hermeneutical phenomenon,' Gadamer points out, 'insofar as its detachment
both from the writer and from a specifically addressed recipient or

reader has given it a life of its own.'[17] Featuring, as it does, both a speaker and an addressee, each enjoying a stable identity (for it is only *within the fiction* that the two rôles are reversed and that Clamence becomes, in his turn, the addressee), the text is apparently not *altogether* that 'kind of alienated speech' whose 'signs need to be transformed back into speech and meaning'[18] since a kind of dialogue has already been entered into or at least the seeds of dialogue have already been sown on fertile soil. What characterizes dialogue is precisely that its language, through the interplay of question and answer, give and take, 'performs that communication of meaning which, with respect to the written tradition, is the task of hermeneutics.'[19] To describe the work of hermeneutics as a conversation with the text is therefore more than a metaphor, 'it is a memory of what originally was the case,'[20] and interpretation hence 'represents the restoration of the original communication of meaning.'[21] Yet, if the addressee, Clamence's fictive interlocutor, is in fact none other than the reader, the speaker is certainly not the author. In order to pursue further the situation I am here concerned with, we must examine closely the fundamental distinction between written language and oral discourse. But first of all, I should point out the importance of this distinction for any discussion of the status of Camus' novelistic texts.

The critics have long debated whether Meursault's story were a kind of diary or the interior monologue of a man condemned to death. In other words, the status of *L'Etranger* as a text lies midway between written language and oral discourse. The one thing that is clear is its very ambiguity in this respect. *La Peste*, on the other hand, leaves no room for doubt: it is, as its very first sentence tells us, a 'chronique' (I, 1217), that is to say a piece of writing. It is no less clear that *La Chute* bears all the traits of the spoken language. The fact that the initial hesitation between the written and the spoken language subsequently gives way to a situation where the written status and oral character respectively of the next two novels are so marked suggests one should pay particular attention to the interplay between the written and the oral in Camus' novelistic texts. If confirmation were needed of this, it is provided by the text of one of his short stories, 'Le Renégat,' the genesis of which was closely intertwined with that of *La Chute*. The oral character of this short text that is, from the beginning, given over to the monologue of a tongueless slave is finally refuted solely by its concluding sentence: 'Une poignée de sel emplit la bouche de l'esclave bavard' (I, 1519), which places the whole of the preceding text, the protagonist's inner monologue, between quotation marks while, at the same time, making of it a written text. By this one sentence, the oral discourse is explicitly transformed into writing and its presence in the short story serves to underline its absence from the text of *La Chute*.

What happens to language when it is written down? Paul Ricœur analyses the radical transformation it undergoes through the writing process in these terms:

The first connection to be altered is that of the message to the speaker. This change indeed is itself one of two symmetrical changes, which affect the interlocutionary situation as a whole. The relation between message and speaker at one end of the communication chain and the relation between message and hearer at the other are together deeply transformed when the face-to-face relation is replaced by the more complex relation of reading to writing, resulting from the direct inscription of discourse in littera.[22]

The result is that the dialogical situation has been, as Ricœur puts it, 'exploded.' With written discourse, the coincidence between the author's mental intention and the verbal meaning of the text ceases to exist and this gives rise to the semantic autonomy of the text that is synonomous with inscription and central to hermeneutics, for exegesis begins with it. This means that 'hermeneutics begins where dialogue ends.'[23]

We have seen that the 'dialogical situation' of oral discourse that is destroyed through its inscription in the form of text appears, in certain respects, to have been restituted and reconstituted through the structure of *La Chute*, which thereby establishes the very conditions for reading, reading being 'concretely accomplished in an act which is, in regard to the text, what speech is in regard to language, namely an event and act of discourse,'[24] and thus brings to the chain of communication that final link that had been dislocated by the inscription of language. But this text of Camus' is already clearly characterized, as remarked earlier, by its oral traits, by the rôle played by shifters, for example. So if it somehow looks ahead to and anticipates its fulfilment as discourse through the hermeneutic activity of the reader, it also continues to bear the imprint of its origins, that is of all language in discourse. It thus manifests, at one and the same time, the desire for what it is not yet and the nostalgia for what it is no longer. Yet, just as its status as dialogue is far from flawless, so its status as oral discourse is also defective and incomplete. What it is lacking is an essential element of oral discourse: the physiological expressivity revealed either through the voice or the body (and particularly through the face and the hands). In this way it rejoins the world of texts to which it belongs once and for all, for, as Gadamer points out, 'in writing, [the] meaning of what is spoken exists purely for itself, completely detached from all emotional elements of expression and communication.'[25]

By this desire and this nostalgia, *La Chute* seems to want to be other than what it is, to escape the condition of all written texts. Language here protests its status as 'alienated discourse.' As text, it never stops working towards this end, taken up by an endeavour that is necessarily doomed to failure. Its defective dialogical structure, precarious because of its lack of equilibrium, bears the most eloquent testimony to the futility of the enterprise.

We have seen that in *La Chute*, as in Camus' first novel, interpretation is thematized and illuminated by the recurring motif of judgment which, through the evocation of the legal process, points to one of the traditional branches of hermeneutics: the study of legal as well as biblical and literary texts. Contrary to the situation in *L'Etranger*, however, this later text does not offer a number of mirror reflections of a given interpretative situation, shimmering at different points on its surface like the convex mirrors of some Dutch paintings. It is not the *product* of interpretation that is its concern but the *process*. It is through its very structure and the dynamic tensions thereby set up within it that it furnishes a model of the hermeneutic act. The workings of this text engage the reader in such a way that he is made aware of the manner in which one necessarily relates to and appropriates, or rather, as Gadamer would say, applies (*Anwendung* rather than *Aneignung*) any text. At the same time, it draws our attention to the predicament all language finds itself in once it is written down and isolated from the rest of the communicative chain of oral discourse that links the speaker to his addressee, taking on a meaning of its own. And what could be more natural since it was precisely as a response to this predicament that the discipline of hermeneutics came into being.

❧6❧

Just between Texts:
Intra-Intertextuality

In the previous chapters, I have spoken of the way the Camusian text functions within itself, produces its own reflection, as well as the way it reproduces within itself its relationship to its reader. It remains to consider the manner in which the different texts relate to one another, for here too a mirroring effect can be seen to be at work. The intertextuality[1] in question is of a very special kind since no texts by other writers are concerned. In fact, if one were to consider the whole of Camus' works as one single text, then one could more accurately speak of 'intra-intertextuality.'[2] It is precisely inasmuch as one does consider his whole literary output as one single text that the mirroring effect involved can be seen to constitute yet another manifestation of formal narcissism. The novelistic texts will remain the focus of my concern, although the texts reflected in them will sometimes be those of Camus' plays.

There can be no doubt that the most striking example of this phenomenon of intra-intertextuality is provided by Camus' first published novel, *L'Etranger*. In the second chapter of the second part, we find the following passage:

Entre ma paillasse et la planche du lit, j'avais trouvé, en effet, un vieux morceau de journal presque collé à l'étoffe, jauni et transparent. Il relatait un fait divers dont le début manquait, mais qui avait dû se passer en Tchécoslovaquie. Un homme était parti d'un village tchèque pour faire fortune. Au bout de vingt-cinq ans, riche, il était revenu avec une femme et un enfant. Sa mère tenait un hôtel avec sa sœur dans son village natal. Pour les surprendre, il avait laissé sa femme et son enfant dans un autre établissement, était allé chez sa mère qui ne l'avait pas reconnu quand il était entré. Par plaisanterie, il avait eu l'idée de prendre une chambre. Il avait montré son argent. Dans la nuit, sa mère et sa sœur l'avaient assassiné à coups de marteau pour le voler et avaient jeté son corps dans la rivière. Le matin, la femme était venue, avait révélé sans le savoir l'identité du voyageur. La mère s'était pendue. La sœur s'était jetée dans un puits. (I, 1180)

Here we have a résumé of the whole dramatic action of Camus' play *Le Malentendu.* My concern is not, of course, with the actual source of this story which has, in fact, been traced to an actual newspaper cutting probably read by the author in Algiers.[3] What is effected by such a reflection of the dramatic text within the novelistic text is that the imaginary world evoked on the stage is taken up within the fictive universe of the novel and thus becomes part of the latter. It should also be noted that a commentary is immediately provided on these events: 'J'ai dû lire cette histoire des milliers de fois. D'un côté, elle était invraisemblable. D'un autre, elle était naturelle. De toute façon, je trouvais que le voyageur l'avait un peu mérité et qu'il ne faut jamais jouer.' (I, 1180) We shall see later the importance and consequences of the existence of such a commentary that is thus set up between these two texts.

Almost as striking as the passage concerning the newspaper cutting is the reflection of Meursault's murder of the Arab in *La Peste*: 'Au milieu d'une conversation animée, [la marchande de tabacs] avait parlé d'une arrestation récente qui avait fait du bruit à Alger. Il s'agissait d'un jeune employé de commerce qui avait tué un Arabe sur la plage.' (I, 1260) As in the last example cited, the fictive events of *L'Etranger* are taken up and drawn into the world of the later novel, making them a part of a fictive universe that is therefore larger and more extensive than that delimited by the text of any one work.[4]

This is, moreover, not by any means the only element carried across from the first novel to the second. Let us recall the journalist who Meursault notices examining him closely 'sans rien exprimer qui fût définissable' and who gives him the impression 'd'être regardé par moi-même.' (I, 1184) Earlier I evoked the possibility of this figure's reflecting the features of the author himself. However, his name could even more likely be Raymond Rambert:

Rieux reçut un jeune homme dont on lui dit qu'il était journaliste ... Il s'appelait Raymond Rambert. Court de taille, les épaules épaisses, le visage décidé, les yeux clairs et intelligents, Rambert portait des habits de coupe sportive et semblait à l'aise dans la vie ... Il enquêtait pour un grand journal de Paris sur les conditions de vie des Arabes ... (I, 1224)

But then neither is Rambert altogether a stranger to Albert Camus, the young Algiers reporter!

More interesting still and wholly unnoticed by the critics to date are the curious resemblances between Tarrou and Meursault. When the narrator of *La Peste* remarks that 'les carnets entament une description détaillée des tramways de notre ville, de leur forme de nacelle, leur couleur indécise, leur saleté habituelle, et terminent ces considérations par un "c'est remarquable" qui n'explique rien' (I, 1236), one could believe he is commenting on Meursault's reactions when, for example, he is asked by Raymond what he thinks of the latter's treatment of the Arab woman, his mistress: 'il voulait savoir ce que je pensais de cette histoire. J'ai répondu que je n'en pensais rien mais que c'était intéressant.' (I, 1145) Meursault's responses are no less unilluminating as far as his feelings or motivation are concerned: 'Lui aussi [Raymond] m'a dit, en parlant de Salamano: "Si c'est pas malheureux!" Il m'a demandé si ça ne me dégoûtait pas et j'ai répondu que non.' (I, 1143) Meursault's constant refrain: '[Raymond] m'a demandé encore si je voulais être son copain. J'ai dit que ça m'était égal ...' (I, 1144), the presence of which we have already noticed earlier in Jonas's conversation, is also taken up by Tarrou:

– Mais sûrement, ce n'est pas contagieux, a-t-il précisé avec empressement. Je lui ai dit que cela m'était égal. (I, 1237)

There is the same non-committal quality to be found in the reactions of Rieux's intriguing companion when his opinion is solicited, as is illustrated by this exchange with the night porter of the hotel:

A l'hôtel, le veilleur de nuit ... m'a dit qu'il s'attendait à un malheur avec tous ces rats. 'Quand les rats quittent le navire ...' Je lui ai répondu que c'était vrai dans le cas des bateaux, mais qu'on ne l'avait jamais vérifié pour les villes.

Cependant, sa conviction est faite. Je lui ai demandé quel malheur, selon lui, on pouvait attendre. Il ne savait pas, le malheur étant impossible à prévoir. Mais il n'aurait pas été étonné qu'un tremblement de terre fit l'affaire. J'ai reconnu que c'était possible ... (I, 1236)

This last response recalls, for example, the Algiers office worker's comment on Salamano's lamentation with regard to his relationship with his dog: 'Il y a huit ans que cela dure. Céleste dit toujours que "c'est malheureux," mais au fond, personne ne peut savoir.' (I, 1142) It is even more curious to note the same mixture of direct and indirect reported speech, the latter in the form of the *discours indirect libre*,[5] and the same alternation between the two in Tarrou's account of the plague as in Meursault's story of his life, as could be seen in the last quotation from *La Peste*. Their turn of phrase, as story-tellers, is strikingly similar. Just as Meursault recounts: '"Voulez-vous, s'est-il exclamé, que ma vie n'ait pas de sens?" A mon avis, cela ne me regardait pas et je le lui ai dit' (I, 1173), so Tarrou narrates: '"– Ah! je vois. Monsieur est comme moi, Monsieur est fataliste." Je n'avais rien avancé de semblable et d'ailleurs je ne suis pas fataliste. Je le lui ai dit ...' (I, 1238) Both characters, moreover, have an eye for the apparently insignificant detail that causes the narrator of *La Peste* to note that Tarrou appears to have opted for 'un parti-pris d'insignifiance' and taken on the rôle of 'l'historien de ce qui n'a pas d'histoire.' (I, 1234) Of Meursault, too, it can often be said, as is said of Tarrou, that he 's'ingénie à considérer les choses et les êtres par le gros bout de la lorgnette' (I, 1234) as when his eyes are drawn to the nails in his mother's coffin: 'On voyait seulement des vis brillantes, à peine enfoncées, se détacher sur les planches passées au brou de noix.' (I, 1127) The description of people who somehow attract their attention has a similarly caricatural quality, whether it be that of the strange little woman in Céleste's café:

J'avais déjà commencé à manger lorsqu'il est entré une bizarre petite femme ... Elle avait des gestes saccadés et des yeux brillants dans une petite figure de pomme. Elle s'est débarrassée de sa jaquette, s'est assise et a consulté fiévreusement la carte. Elle a appelé Céleste et a commandé immédiatement tous ses plats d'une voix à la fois précise et précipitée ... elle a ... sorti de son sac un crayon bleu et un magazine qui donnait les programmes radiophoniques de la semaine. Avec beaucoup de soin, elle a coché une à une presque toutes les émissions. Comme le magazine avait une douzaine de pages, elle a continué ce travail méticuleusement pendant tout le repas. J'avais déjà fini qu'elle cochait encore avec la même application. Puis elle s'est levée, a remis sa jaquette avec les mêmes gestes précis d'automate et elle est partie. (I, 1155)

Or the family Tarrou is fascinated by in the hôtel restaurant:

Au restaurant de l'hôtel, il y a toute une famille bien intéressante. Le père est un grand homme maigre, habillé de noir, avec un col dur. Il a le milieu du crâne chauve et deux touffes de cheveux gris, à droite et à gauche. Des petits yeux ronds et durs, un nez mince, une bouche horizontale, lui donnent l'air d'une chouette bien élevée. Il arrive toujours le premier à la porte du restaurant, s'efface, laisse passer sa femme, menue comme une souris noire, et entre alors avec, sur les talons, un petit garçon et une petite fille habillés comme des chiens savants. Arrivé à sa table, il attend que sa femme ait pris place, s'assied, et les deux caniches peuvent enfin se percher sur leurs chaises. Il dit 'vous' à sa femme et à ses enfants, débite des méchancetés polies à la première et des paroles définitives aux héritiers ...

Les deux caniches ont piqué le nez dans leur pâtée et la chouette a remercié d'un signe de tête qui n'en disait pas long. (I, 1236-7)

The range of reflections we have been looking at in this comparison between Tarrou and Meursault is of such a nature that the phenomenon in question is clearly different from what has been considered so far in this chapter. Some distinctions are called for at this point. The present examples clearly have nothing in common with the 'content' or substance of the fiction, the events related (except marginally in the case of the evocation of the two restaurant scenes), but rather with the *manner* of their telling. They do not therefore create a kind of fusion or potential merging together of the fictive universes of the two texts, although such an effect is, of course, created by the evocation of the murder of the Arab on the beach in Algiers by the minor character quoted earlier. Nor, at first sight, do they permit one to give full rein to one's imagination by postulating a rôle, although unseen and unheard, for Tarrou within the world of Meursault's experience, as I was tempted to do earlier for Rambert, which is another more fanciful, or at least more debatable and perhaps gratuitous way of effecting the merging of the fictions of two distinct novelistic texts.

The fact of the matter is that, when viewed from our present rather particular and unusual perspective, the two characters of Meursault et Tarrou are, in a sense, mutually exclusive precisely because they are so similar. For this reason, they could not be seen as co-existing within the same fictive universe. But are their similarities such as to lead one to consider them to be one and the same character? Most readers, I think, would have no hesitation in answering that question in the negative, given the striking contrast between Tarrou's lucidity and rather intellectual nature, on the one hand, and Meursault's disingenuousness on the other. The fact that no similarities at all have generally been perceived between the two is already answer enough – unless one could see in Tarrou a Meursault who had escaped the death penalty and developed his newfound awareness dating from his outburst against the prison chaplain in his cell. After all, doesn't Tarrou say of his past existence:

Quand j'étais jeune, je vivais avec l'idée de mon innocence, c'est-à-dire avec pas d'idée du tout. Je n'ai pas le genre tourmenté, j'ai débuté comme il convenait. Tout me réussissait, j'étais à l'aise dans l'intelligence, au mieux avec les femmes, et si j'avais quelques inquiétudes, elles passaient comme elles étaient venues. Un jour, j'ai commencé à réfléchir. Maintenant ... (I, 1418)

Could this reflection not have been sparked off by his experience in a death cell? However, such an hypothesis is not supported by the one real thematic link between the two novels: the theme of capital punishment and the legal system. Tarrou recounts how, at the age of seventeen, he went for the first time to hear his father, a lawyer, plead in court:

Je n'ai pourtant gardé de cette journée qu'une seule image, celle du coupable. Je crois qu'il était coupable en effet, il importe peu de quoi. Mais ce petit homme au poil roux et pauvre, d'une trentaine d'années, paraissait si décidé à tout reconnaître, si sincèrement effrayé par ce qu'il avait fait et ce qu'on allait lui faire, qu'au bout de quelques minutes je n'eus plus d'yeux que pour lui. Il avait l'air d'un hibou effarouché par une lumière trop vive. Le nœud de sa cravate ne

s'ajustait pas exactement à l'angle du col. Il se rongeait les ongles d'une seule main, la droite ... Bref, je n'insiste pas, vous avez compris qu'il était vivant.
(I, 1419-20)

However, at best, one could imagine that it was Meursault himself who had been in the dock that day – except, of course, that the latter, while doubtless appearing gauche to the onlooker, was certainly not contrite or frightened. Tarrou is clearly, if anywhere in the picture, on the other side of the fence, as his easy familiarity with and acceptance of the legal terms and procedures contrast with Meursault's contrary attitude to the latter. This we see from the continuation of his tale:

Mais moi, je m'en apercevais brusquement, alors que, jusqu'ici, je n'avais pensé à lui qu'à travers la catégorie commode d'"inculpé." Je ne puis dire que j'oubliais alors mon père, mais quelque chose me serrait le ventre qui m'enlevait toute autre attention que celle que je portais au prévenu. Je n'écoutais presque rien, je sentais qu'on voulait tuer cet homme vivant et un instinct formidable comme une vague me portait à ses côtés avec une sorte d'aveuglement entêté. (I, 1420)

Thus, in spite of the similarities in the rhetoric of their depiction of the trial scene:

Et je compris qu'il demandait la mort de cet homme au nom de la société et qu'il demandait même qu'on lui coupât le cou. Il disait seulement, il est vrai: 'Cette tête doit tomber.' Mais, à la fin, la différence n'était pas grande. Et cela revint au même, en effet, puisqu'il obtint cette tête. Simplement, ce n'est pas lui qui fit alors le travail. (I, 1420)

Tarrou is not to be confused, as a character, with Meursault, past, present, or future.

What, then, are we to make of these myriad reflections of Camus' first novel centred around Tarrou's tale? Or, to express things in a more fruitful manner, what is their effect on the functioning of the texts in question, what is the part they play in the general textual economy of *La Peste*? The beginnings of an answer to this question are to be found by recalling the passage quoted earlier where Tarrou refers to spending Sunday afternoon on one's balcony as one of the ways of not wasting one's time (cf. I, 1235). Such a remark appears as a kind of retroactive commentary on what is clearly one of Meursault's characteristic activities, typical of his life-style. The same is true of the account of the rôle played by telegrams during the epidemic of the plague:

Les télégrammes restèrent alors notre seule ressource. Des êtres que liaient l'intelligence, le cœur et la chair, en furent réduits à chercher les signes de cette communion dans les majuscules d'une dépêche de dix mots. Et comme, en fait, les formules qu'on peut utiliser dans un télégramme sont vite épuisées, de longues vies communes ou des passions douloureuses se résumèrent rapidement dans un échange de formules toutes faites comme: 'Vais bien. Pense à toi. Tendresse.' (I, 1272)

Does this not provide a very eloquent commentary on the opening paragraph of *L'Etranger*? 'Aujourd'hui, maman est morte. Ou peut-être hier, je ne sais pas. J'ai reçu un télégramme de l'asile: "Mère décédée. Enterrement demain. Sentiments distingués." Cela ne veut rien dire. C'était peut-être hier.' (I, 1125) In the light of the former passage, Meursault's disturbing 'Cela ne veut rien dire' takes on a quite unambiguous, reassuringly reasonable meaning. That would be an end to the matter – if only Meursault, rather than Tarrou, had penned the lines in question! But he didn't. So what would have been part of any coherent, over-all interpretation of the Algiers office worker becomes something quite different: the commentary of one *text* upon another *text*.

That this type of reflection operates on the level of the text rather than being, in any sense, dependent on the coherence and cohesion of the fiction can be usefully illustrated by another of the entries from Tarrou's diary, whose words were 'les premiers qui fussent personnels': 'Ma mère était ainsi, j'aimais en elle le même effacement et c'est elle que j'ai toujours voulu rejoindre. Il y a huit ans, je ne peux pas dire qu'elle soit morte. Elle s'est seulement effacée un peu plus que d'habitude et, quand je me suis retourné, elle n'était pas là.' (I, 1444) Although it is true that Meursault does, at the beginning of his story, use the words: 'Pour le moment, c'est un peu comme si maman n'étais pas morte' (I, 1125), the most striking reflection we have here is of the ending of Salamano's account of how he lost his dog: 'Je me suis arrêté pour regarder "le Roi de l'Evasion." Et quand j'ai voulu repartir, il n'était plus là.' (I, 1151) Only a close psychoanalytical reading[6] of *L'Etranger* reveals the parallel between, on the one hand, the couple formed by Salamano and his dog and, on the other, the relationship between Meursault and his mother!

But let us return to the question of the function of the passages quoted from Tarrou's diary in relation to the text of Camus' first novel. I have already noted that the reflections operate more on the level of the manner events are related than on that of the nature of the events themselves and concern therefore the style of the narrative rather than the fiction. This suggests the most obvious parallel of all: the fact that both Meursault and Tarrou are writers of diaries – or are they? Tarrou certainly is, even though his diary is referred to by the narrator as a kind of 'chronicle.' (I, 1234) But haven't I already been at pains earlier to stress the ambiguity of the status of Meursault's story and the impossibility of deciding whether it is a diary or an inner monologue? Here precisely, I believe, lies the key to the resemblances between the two texts. In a nutshell, it is my contention that Tarrou's diary is none other than a *re*production by the text of *La Peste* of the whole text of the earlier novel. At one and the same time, the text of *L'Etranger* is thereby taken up in a reflected and refracted form by the later text and has its status resolved retroactively. This belated and yet significant resolution is effected in two ways: firstly and most obviously, because its reflection is clearly designated as a diary and secondly and more interestingly, because it now lies embedded within this new text, its contours clearly and definitively delimited by the latter, which effectively places it within quotation marks.

The resulting configuration of the text of *La Peste* is therefore even more remarkable in its complexity than that sketched out in Chapter 2. The process of *mise-en-abyme*, or at least *enchâssement*, that was there seen to end up by turning itself inside out is now seen to encompass, without losing its curious *intra*textual circularity, an *inter*textual dimension. It is not only Tarrou's chronicle that is embedded within Rieux's but also the text of Meursault's tale which is to be read as a palimpsest. In other words, Tarrou's story inasmuch as it is a chronicle points to and reflects that other chronicle that encompasses it and inasmuch as it is a diary, it refers to and constitutes a curious retroactive interpretation of *L'Etranger*.

The manner in which we find a curious focusing of certain salient features of Meursault's tale in the extracts from Tarrou's diary in *La Peste* whereby the former finally takes on the attributes of a written text recalls the discussion in Chapter 5 of the commentary furnished by the formal characteristics of 'Le Renégat' upon the formal status of *La Chute*. The embedding of the reflection of *L'Etranger* in *La Peste* closes off the earlier work within quotation marks just as surely as the final sentence of 'Le Renégat' creates a retroactive framing of the whole preceding text, while at the same time having the effect of highlighting the absence of such quotation marks around that other monologue attributed not to the renegade but to Clamence. In both cases, the reflection of one text in the other sets up a dialectical relationship between the two, a reciprocal commentary which operates as a kind of interpretative process through which the texts interpret one another. (This purely internal self-interpretation by the total canon of the writer's works brings to mind an analogous situation in the work of a writer who greatly influenced Camus, André Gide,[7] except that the author of *L'Immoraliste* explicitly postulated such a state of affairs in stressing the complementarity of the latter text, for example, and *La Porte étroite*.) In both cases, too, the import of the commentary thus articulated concerns the formal status of the texts in question and, in particular, the problematics of the relationship between the written language and oral discourse, the first giving rise to a self-contained text constituting a closed system and the second to an act of discourse or the model of the hermeneutic process.

In Chapter 5, I did not, however, exhaust all the pertinent factors operative, in this respect, in the relationship between 'Le Renégat' and *La Chute*. Even before the last sentence arrives to both fill the mouth of the slave with 'une poignée de sel' (I, 1591), thereby effectively putting an end to his verbal ramblings, and formally close off the preceding monologue with quotation marks, another crucial aspect of the short story is not without its pertinence here. 'Je suis bavard, hélas ...' (I, 1476), exclaims Clamence: 'C'est le trop plein; dès que j'ouvre la bouche, les phrases coulent.' (I, 1480) Likewise, the protagonist of 'Le Renégat' is explicitly designated as a gossip by the text itself as it finally declares its own existence independent of the hero of its fiction: 'Une poignée de sel emplit la bouche de l'esclave bavard.' (I, 1591) How apt a designation, the reader says to himself. But is it? In fact he is faced with exactly the same situation as when he had been encouraged to remark the apparently common rôle of diarist filled both by Tarrou and Meursault. The point about gossips is surely that they are never at a loss for words and never lose their tongue, whereas such has been precisely the fate of the unfortunate renegade-priest! The latter is as unlikely a gossip as Meursault is an unlikely diarist![8] Here the dialectical relationship between the two texts is no less revealing and significant than that existing between Camus' first two novels. And just as, in this respect, the structure of the short story comments, as we have seen, on the essentially oral characteristics of *La Chute* and its open-ended structure, so the text of the latter reveals the problematic nature of the renegade's apparent monologue.

The importance of physiological expressivity, whether it be through the voice, the hands, or the face, in conferring on oral discourse its essential specificity in contrast to the written language was already noted in the last chapter. With the loss of his tongue, the protagonist of 'Le Renégat' has lost all possibility of that expressivity that our words acquire through being voiced, in other words all emotive colour that comes from the tonality of the human voice. The result is a dimunition in communicability:

Quelle bouille, quelle bouillie! Il faut mettre de l'ordre dans ma tête. Depuis qu'ils m'ont coupé la langue, une autre langue, je ne sais pas, marche sans arrêt dans mon crâne, quelque chose parle, ou quelqu'un qui se tait soudain et puis tout recommence, ô j'entends trop de choses que je ne dis pourtant pas, quelle bouillie, et si j'ouvre la bouche, c'est comme un bruit de cailloux remués. (I, 1578)

The main indication within the text of this loss of communicability is furnished by the 'râ râ' with which it is punctuated from time to time and which thwarts the production of meaning by reducing it to a state of incomprehensible incoherence. The ostensibly oral discourse is already seriously flawed by this lack of expressivity, as flawed, in fact, as the character is physically handicapped. More significantly still, the very possibility of an oral monologue is definitively ruled out since what would it be uttered with? The apparent monologue is therefore revealed for the 'fiction' it necessarily is, but doubly so, for even within the fiction, its status as discourse is completely lacking in credibility. One would, in fact, in order to preserve the coherence of the fiction, have to presume that the renegade had recourse to pen and paper to express himself. But then, in that case, the text of the main body of the short story (that is to say without its final sentence) could not have the status of a monologue at all, since even the possibility of an *inner* monologue, as opposed to an orally articulated one, would be eliminated and it would already have taken on the form of transcribed language or text. In conclusion, the emasculation of the protagonist, in addition to the Freudian overtones of castration,[9] already point to the formal resolution of the text occasioned by its concluding sentence, the existence of which calls into being nothing less than a '*pre*narrator' in the manner of *La Peste*. It cannot operate effectively as oral discourse and its defective nature already reveals the shortcomings of all language once it is congealed in the written word. It is, as it were, predestined to become text and to close in on itself. In fact, what is even more curious is that the consequent status of this voiceless monologue is such that it ends up by taking on precisely that ambiguity that characterizes *L'Etranger*, being neither fish nor fowl, neither monologue nor diary.

I explored earlier, in Chapter 3, the considerable interplay that exists between *La Chute* and the text of 'Jonas.' In this connection, I had occasion to exploit the term coined by Roland Barthes, *texte étoilé*, and suggested that the short story, which was revealed to be the text produced by the star, by *l'étoile* both as signifier and signified, and hence a *texte-étoile*, functions precisely as a *texte étoilé* in that it could also be seen to disintegrate and break down into fragments that it shared, through the by now familiar mirroring effect symptomatic of all forms of autorepresentation, with the texts of *L'Etranger* as well as *La Chute*, as though linking up with the latter through the far-reaching effect of the star's rays. However, since the relationship between the two texts is necessarily reciprocal, one could equally well extend and modify the image of the star and its wondrous textual effects, by pointing out that just as its rays reach out to make contact with *La Chute*, the text of the novel picks up the starlight, refracts and reflects it, as it plays on its surface. For 'Jonas' is not the only Camusian text that is mirrored in and by *La Chute*.

From the present particular perspective of intra-intertextuality, it is not altogether fanciful to picture the text of *La Chute* as one of those multifaceted revolving glass globes in a dance-hall, the facets of which reflect other texts. This is the case with 'Le Renégat' in spite of the most complex interplay with this text examined earlier. The sado-masochism of the master-slave relationship that the renegade-priest ends up by luxuriating in is to be found inscribed directly in the form of Clamence's relationship with his mistress, who had 'confié à un tiers [ses] insuffisances':

Je revis un peu plus tard cette femme, je fis ce qu'il fallait pour la séduire et la reprendre vraiment. Ce ne fut pas très difficile: elles non plus n'aiment pas rester sur un échec. Dès cet instant, sans le vouloir clairement, je me mis, en fait, à la mortifier de toutes les façons. Je l'abandonnais et la reprenais, la forçais à se donner dans des temps et des lieux qui ne s'y prêtaient pas, la traitais de façon si brutale, dans tous les domaines, que je finis par m'attacher à elle comme j'imagine que le geôlier se lie à son prisonnier. Et cela jusqu'au jour où, dans le violent désordre d'un plaisir douloureux et contraint, elle rendit hommage à voix haute à ce qui l'asservissait. (I, 1506)

The same is true of Clamence's words in praise of the brotherhood of collective servitude:

Quand nous serons tous coupables, ce sera la démocratie. Sans compter, cher ami, qu'il faut se venger de devoir mourir seul. La mort est solitaire tandis que la servitude est collective. Les autres ont leur compte aussi, et en même temps que nous, voilà l'important. Tous réunis, enfin, mais à genoux, et la tête courbée. (I, 1543)

It is not surprising to find that that other work concerned with sadism, arbitrary power, and collective subjugation, *Caligula*, also plays on the surface of the text of Camus' last novel at several points. The solution Clamence would be tempted by is realized by the Roman Emperor: 'Mais on ne peut souhaiter la mort de tout le monde, ni, à la limite, dépeupler la planète pour jouir d'une liberté inimaginable autrement.' (I, 1508) Since 'chacun exige d'être innocent à tout prix, même si, pour cela, il faut accuser le genre humain et le ciel.' (I, 1515) The only way to attain this end is clearly perceived by Clamence: 'L'essentiel est que tout devienne simple, comme pour l'enfant ... que le bien et le mal soient désignés de façon arbitraire, donc évidente.' (I, 1543)

In the case of Camus' first novel, the reflections of that text become refractions. If the Meursault of the first part of *L'Etranger* could well have exclaimed: 'N'était-ce pas cela, en effet, l'Eden, cher monsieur: la vie en prise directe? Ce fut la mienne. Je n'ai jamais eu besoin d'apprendre à vivre' (I, 1487), and if he could easily have offered the following commentary on his existence:

Je vivais donc sans autre continuité que celle, au jour le jour, du moi-moi-moi. Au jour le jour les femmes, au jour le jour la vertu ou le vice, au jour le jour, comme les chiens, mais tous les jours, moi-même, solide au poste. J'avançais ainsi à la surface de la vie, dans les mots en quelque sorte, jamais dans la réalité. (I, 1499)

Nonetheless the rude awakening brought about by the consequences of his killing of the Arab is far from resulting in Clamence's lucid cynicism. The latter's consequent feeling of culpability, although expressed in terms that directly reflect Meursault's experience, was present from the beginning in the make-up of the hero of *L'Etranger*:

Mes rapports avec mes contemporains étaient les mêmes, en apparence, et pourtant devenaient subtilement désaccordés ... je me sentais vulnérable, et livré à l'accusation publique. Mes semblables cessaient d'être à mes yeux l'auditoire respectueux dont j'avais l'habitude. Le cercle dont j'étais le centre se brisait et ils se plaçaient sur une seule rangée, comme au tribunal. (I, 1513)

In fact, the same complexity emerges from any careful scrutiny of the relationship between these two texts[10] as emerged from the discussion above of Tarrou and Meursault. The affinities between Meursault and the 'bon sauvage' have been noted by many a critic:[11]

Non seulement je ne risquais pas de rejoindre le camp des criminels (en particulier, je n'avais aucune chance de tuer ma femme, étant célibataire), mais encore je prenais leur défense, à la seule condition qu'ils fussent de bons meurtriers, comme d'autres sont de bons sauvages. (I, 1483)

What is, however, suggested by this last passage is not that Clamence can be mistaken for Meursault, but rather that Meursault could well have been one of the Parisian lawyer's clients, since what better example of a 'bon meurtrier' can there be than an 'innocent' murderer such as that 'seul christ que nous méritions' (I, 1921), as his creator called him? What is more, as in the case of the character of the journalist Rambert earlier in this chapter, a certain Albert Camus, in his rôle as author of *L'Etranger*, cannot be altogether lost sight of when one reads the following: 'J'apprenais du moins que je n'étais du côté des coupables, des accusés, que dans la mesure exacte où leur faute ne me causait aucun dommage. Leur culpabilité me rendait éloquent parce que je n'en étais pas la victime.' (I, 1502) Was not that eloquent case he made out for his 'bon meurtrier' Meursault only convincing inasmuch as the reader was encouraged to forget the very existence of the victim, not to mention the fact that the latter just happened to be an Arab?[12]

Reflections of Camus' second novel in *La Chute* are less common and certainly less obvious. Here again it is more a question of refraction than reflection. Once one takes into account the symbolic character of *La Peste* as a scarcely veiled allegory of the German occupation of France during the Second World War,[13] the pertinence for the present discussion of Clamence's disturbing comments on the Nazis' extermination of the Jews becomes clear:

Moi, j'habite le quartier juif, ou ce qui s'appelait ainsi jusqu'au moment où nos frères hitlériens y ont fait de la place. Quel lessivage! Soixante-quinze mille juifs déportés ou assassinés, c'est le nettoyage par le vide. J'admire cette application, cette méthodique patience. o (I, 1479)

This immediately brings to mind the attempts made by the narrator of *La Peste* to imagine the number of the plague's victims:

Dix mille morts font cinq fois le public d'un grand cinéma. Voilà ce qu'il faudrait faire. On rassemble les gens à la sortie de cinq cinémas, on les conduit sur une place de la ville et on les fait mourir en tas pour y voir un peu clair. Au moins, on pourrait mettre alors des visages connus sur cet entassement anonyme. (I, 1246)

There is also the occasional mirror image of a rhetorical turn of phrase as when Clamence remarks: 'la confession de mes fautes me permet de recommencer plus légèrement et de jouir deux fois, de ma nature d'abord, et ensuite d'un charmant repentir' (I, 1546), which appears to echo Rieux's comment on the plight of Oran's inhabitants: 'En fait, nous souffrions deux fois – de notre souffrance d'abord et de celle ensuite que nous imaginions aux absents, fils, épouse ou amante.' (I, 1274) The refraction that takes place in the passage from one text to the other can be appreciated from the two following examples. Clamence's scathing account of his scandalising 'nos humanistes professionnels' (I, 1520) has a cutting edge to it that Rieux's gentle, humorous understatement lacks: 'Nos concitoyens à cet égard étaient comme tout le monde, ils pensaient à eux-mêmes, autrement dit ils étaient humanistes: ils ne croyaient pas aux fléaux.' (I, 1245) In the same way, the statement that 'A Oran comme ailleurs, faute de temps et de réflexion, on est bien obligé de s'aimer sans le savoir' (I, 1218) becomes the following far less subtle affirmation: 'Bien entendu, le véritable amour est exceptionnel, deux ou trois fois par siècle à peu près. Le reste du temps, il y a la vanité ou l'ennui.' (I, 1503) In short, irony is reflected as sarcasm and subtlety gives way to the discordantly obvious.

These last examples, as well as reflections in *La Chute* of 'Le Renégat' and *Caligula* cited earlier, are in the brief and succinct form of maxim-like statements and as such are perhaps the only aspect of stylistic continuity between Clamence's pseudo-confession and the narration of the events of the plague. As this feature is charac-teristic of the stylistic texture of Camus' last novel in general, it should come as no surprise to realize that maxim-like statements play an important rôle in the intertextuality of *La Chute*. The significance of this state of affairs is not, however, inconsiderable. First of all, it explains my recourse to the apparently extravagant image of a multi-faceted glass globe to describe the status of this text in its interplay with other texts. Each of the maxims corresponds, as it were, to one of the many reflecting facets of the sphere. Like these innumerable facets that do not make up a smooth, unbroken surface, maxims do not link up with one another but constitute a sequence of discontinuous general truths bearing only a very tangential relationship to a coherent fictive universe with its own specificity. They do not, in fact, have any direct part in the evocation of the fiction as such and belong as much, if not more, to the domain of the essay than to that of the novel. This brings us to a second more important consequence. It is that the reflections of other texts are both very limited in their scope and superficial, shimmering on the surface of the text without engaging it in any depth, like so much light playing on the glass globe. This means that no real intertextual dialogue develops, as it did between *La Peste* and *L'Etranger*. Lastly, the sheer number of the reflections, as well as the number of different Camusian works reflected (which are far from having been exhausted in these pages), adds credence to the superficiality of the phenomenon, not without, however, pointing to the very particular status of *La Chute* in drawing together within its confines so much of the substance of the thematics of the whole Camusian canon. All the texts are, in a sense, reworked in the working-out of this most remarkable of texts which casts a disturbing light on its predecessors.[14] In precisely what way they are reworked is what remains to be explored in this chapter.

In the main body of this book I have not been concerned with the actual chronology of Camus' works of fiction, the sequence of their publication, as can be seen from the chapter titles, with *L'Etranger* (1942) following *La Peste* (1947) and 'Jonas' (1957), because my interest has not been centred upon the evolution of a writer, Albert Camus, but rather on the internal functioning of his texts. The specific formal properties of the latter already suggested the logic that has determined the ordering of the chapters. Moreover, from the present point of view focusing on textual productivity and the internal generation of the text, as opposed to the historical genesis of the manuscript, the diachronic is necessarily subordinated to the synchronic, historical precedence to contiguity in the present of the reader and critic. It is precisely the co-existence of the various texts that sanctions the study of their interaction as undertaken in the preceding pages. At the same time, however, the results of the analysis suggest that now is the time to introduce into the discussion the diachronic dimension, since the dialectical relationship set up between the different texts by their internal workings does point to a dynamic evolution going from the first to the last texts. My remark earlier that the ambiguous status of 'Le Renégat' appears to reproduce the analogous status of *L'Etranger* with its hesitation between the diary form and the inner monologue already suggests as much, opening up as it does the possibility of a distinct symmetry between the earlier text and one of the latest.

As one moves from *L'Etranger* to *La Peste* and thence to *La Chute*, examining each in relation to the rest of Camus' works as well as in relation to one another, one has the impression of two contrary and complementary movements: a closing-in or systole effect and an opening-out or diastole effect. The first, centripetal in character, marks the transition from his first to his second novel and results in an increased stress on the written text and autoreferentiality. The second, centrifugal in character, characterizes the transition from *La Peste* to *La Chute* with the accent shifting onto oral discourse and the process of autorepresentation encompassing within itself the act of reading and interpreting.

We have seen how the text of *L'Etranger* appeared to be taken up within *La Peste* in the form of Tarrou's diary and endowed retroactively with all the attributes of the written text. Let us not lose sight of the fact that the fictive diary, the novel in diary form, is already in itself an autorepresentation inasmuch as it is a book within a book[15] where there is paradoxically no overlap of the former by the latter, no embedding of the one within the other, since the two are identical, sharing the same textual boundaries. One book, a novel, does not reproduce within its fiction another book, a diary, but itself constitutes a representation of the latter. The same is true of the whole text of *La Peste* precisely because it is designated as a chronicle and the fictive chronicle has, in this respect, a status analogous to that of the fictive diary. Just as *L'Etranger* encapsulated in the form of a short text from a newspaper the story of a play, *Le Malentendu*, so *La Peste*, in its turn, not only places quotation marks around the whole of the preceding novelistic text with the quotations from Tarrou's diary but also cites the actual events of *L'Etranger* with its mention of the murder of the Arab on the beach by the young office worker (cf. I, 1260). In other words, *La Peste* not only categorically affirms its own status as a written text but also gathers together and reproduces other works such as *L'Etranger* and, indirectly, *Le Malentendu*, thereby reducing them to the status of so many documents to be placed alongside those drawn upon and cited by the chronicler Rieux. Through the workings of intertextuality, these other texts themselves become comprised within the field of autoreferentiality exemplified by *La Peste* where the text becomes a self-contained, closed system endlessly reflecting (upon) itself. The shift here from the situation of the text of Camus' first novel, which intimately and inextricably involved its reader and his reading by reflecting and refracting the latter's own interpretation of the work, is obvious.

The subsequent movement resulting in the text of *La Chute* tends to reverse the previous evolution. For while this last novel of Camus' also interacts, as we have seen, with a number of other texts such as 'Jonas,' 'Le Renégat,' *Caligula*, *L'Etranger*, and *La Peste*, these other works are reflected within a text that is an open-ended structure rather than a closed system, a text that attempts to incarnate the dialogical structure of the act of discourse and restitute to language those properties that all language loses through its inscription. Nothing better demonstrates this process than the interplay analysed above between *La Chute* and 'Le Renégat,' and did not the text of the short story already reveal at work within itself the same tension between the written and the spoken? These other works thereby lose the quotation marks that were placed around them by *La Peste* and conferred upon them their status as written documents as they become, as it were, reactivated within the hermeneutic model itself as constituted by *La Chute*. The systole gives way to the diastole and the centripetal to the centrifugal. And while the shift from the reflection of the reader's interpretation on the text in *L'Etranger* to the reflection of the text itself in a wholly narcissistic fashion in *La Peste* is, in a sense, reversed, the reflection is no longer solely on the level of representation through the evocation of mirrors[16] in different forms, as in Camus' first novel, but on that of the whole structure and functioning of the text that acts out, as it were, and initiates the whole hermeneutic process whereby the reader appropriates each and every text.

Through this account of the intra-intertextuality of Camus' fiction we can glimpse a renewal, in the contemporary context, of an old and by now largely discredited concept, that of an author's complete works, his *œuvres complètes*. As Tzvetan Todorov has pointed out, the latter concept has become distinctly problematical[17] once one no longer considers literary works as some kind of emanation from and expression of their author. It is, in fact, impossible, in my view, to give any credence to such a concept without having recourse to the author as creator whose existence can alone sanction it, as he constitutes the only common denominator between the various texts. In those works constituted by the collected fiction of, say, a Balzac which features the phenomenon of recurring characters common to more than one novel, it is true that the texts of the different novels do come together but the result is a new text that forms an aesthetic unit in itself, analogous to that of any cyclical novel. The merging of the different fictive universes, of *L'Etranger* and *Le Malentendu*, of *La Peste* and *La Chute*, evoked above is of a different kind, as is indicated by the difficulties encountered in attempting to recognize the features of a Meursault in those of Tarrou.

Rather than finding either characters or their fictive worlds living on in subsequent novels, we are confronted by a wholly different process that is characteristic of the activity of the particular phenomenon of text: the act of quoting. One text quotes other texts which thereby become part of a new textual economy. Thus while we have been able to observe, in previous chapters, the diverse ways in which the text reflects upon itself, when it does look beyond itself, reflecting and referring to another text, it is nonetheless still indulging in that propensity to which all texts are, by their very nature, prone: narcissism. The world of texts is a world of mirrors, as self-contained as a kaleidoscope.

Notes

INTRODUCTION

1 See Brian T. Fitch, *Essai de bibliographie des études en langue française consacrées à Albert Camus (1937-62)* (Paris: Lettres Modernes 1965), and subsequent editions in collaboration with Peter C. Hoy (2nd edition, 1969, covering the period 1937-67, and 3rd edition, 1972, covering the period 1937-70) for criticism on Camus in French. For criticism in all languages, see Robert C. Roeming, *Camus: A Bibliography* (Madison: University of Wisconsin Press 1968), and the bibliographies published in the annual 'Albert Camus' volumes of *La Revue des Lettres Modernes*, ed. Brian T. Fitch, since 1968.

2 Cf. Peter Cryle, *Bilan critique: 'L'Exil et le royaume' d'Albert Camus: essai d'analyse* (Paris: Lettres Modernes 1973), and *Albert Camus* 6, 'Camus nouvelliste: L'Exil et le royaume' (1973).

3 See 'Bibliographie critique' 157-73 in Brian T. Fitch, *'L'Etranger' d'Albert Camus: un texte, ses lecteurs, leurs lectures* (Paris: Larousse 1972). For a review of all criticism devoted to Camus' fiction, see my annual 'Recensement et recension des articles: romans, nouvelles, études esthétiques' in the 'Albert Camus' volumes.

4 Cf. Robert Champigny, *Sur un héros païen* (Paris: Gallimard 1959); Brian T. Fitch, *Narrateur et narration dans 'L'Etranger' d'Albert Camus* (Paris: Lettres Modernes 1960) (2nd revised and enlarged edition, 1968); M.-G. Barrier, *L'Art du récit dans 'L'Etranger' d'Albert Camus* (Paris: Nizet 1962); Pierre-Georges Castex, *Albert Camus et 'L'Etranger'* (Paris: Corti 1965); Pierre-Louis Rey, *Camus: 'L'Etranger'* (Paris: Hatier 1970); Bernard Pingaud, *'L'Etranger' de Camus* (Paris: Hachette 1971); Fitch, *'L'Etranger' d'Albert Camus: un texte, ses lecteurs, leurs lectures* (Paris: Larousse 1972); G.V. Banks, *Camus: 'L'Etranger'* (London: Edward

Arnold 1976); Rosemarie Jones, *Camus, 'L'Etranger' and 'La Chute'* (London: Grant and Cutler Ltd 1980).

5 Cf. Donald Haggis, *Camus: 'La Peste'* (Woodbury, NY: Barron's Educational Series, Inc. 1962); Pol Gaillard, *Camus: 'La Peste'* (Paris: Hatier 1972); *Albert Camus* 8, 'Camus romancier: *La Peste*' (1976).

6 This was particularly true of the earlier criticism on *L'Etranger* that saw this novel as a direct illustration of the 'absurd' as expounded in *Le Mythe de Sisyphe*. See my critique of such criticism in 'Sartre et *L'Etranger*' and '*L'Etranger* et l'absurde' 5-9 and 10-5 in *Narrateur et narration* ..., 1st edition 1960.

7 Cf. Jean-Paul Sartre, 'Explication de *L'Etranger*,' *Cahiers du sud* 253 (1943) 189-206 (reprinted in *Situations I* [Paris: Gallimard 1947] 99-121); Haydn T. Mason, 'Voltaire and Camus,' *The Romanic Review* LIX 3 (Oct. 1968) 198-212; and Patrick Henry, *Voltaire and Camus: The Limits of Reason and the Awareness of Absurdity* (Banbury, Oxfordshire: The Voltaire Foundation, 'Studies on Voltaire and the Eighteenth Century' 1975). For details of comparative studies devoted to Camus, see Brian T. Fitch and Peter C. Hoy, 'Bibliographie des études comparatives,' *Albert Camus* 4 (1971) 287-323, and Peter C. Hoy, 'Complément et supplément aux études comparatives,' *Albert Camus* 5 (1972) 285-98.

8 Cf. Brian T. Fitch, *'L'Etranger' d'Albert Camus: un texte* ... 155-6.

9 Cf. *Albert Camus* 3, 'Sur *La Chute*' (1970); Pierre-Louis Rey, *Camus: 'La Chute'* (Paris: Hatier 1970); Phan Thi Ngoc Mai, *De la responsabilité selon 'La Chute' d'Albert Camus* (Saigon: Les Presses de Kim Lai An Quan 1971) (limited edition of a thesis presented to the Faculté des Lettres de Saigon); Claudine et Michel Maillard, *Le Langage en procès: structures et symboles dans 'La Chute' de Camus* (Grenoble: Presses Universitaires de Grenoble 1977); Jones, *Camus, 'L'Etranger' and 'La Chute'*; and Yves Reuter, *Texte/Idéologie dans 'La Chute' de Camus* (Paris: Lettres Modernes 1980). For a review of the criticism devoted to *La Chute* up to 1970, see '*La Chute* et ses lecteurs. I. Jusqu'en 1962 (by André Abbou) II. Depuis 1962 (by Brian T. Fitch)' 9-19 and 20-32 in *Albert Camus* 3 (1970).

10 Cf. Albert Camus, 'Lettre au Directeur des *Temps Modernes*,' *Les Temps modernes* 82 (août 1952) 317-33; Jean-Paul Sartre, 'Réponse à Albert Camus,' *ibid.* 334-53; Francis Jeanson, 'Pour tout vous dire,' *ibid.* 354-83.

11 Cf. 'La réception de *L'Etranger*' 11-15 in *'L'Etranger' d'Albert Camus: un texte* ...

12 Cf. Fitch, *Narrateur et narration* ..., Barrier, *L'Art du récit dans 'L'Etranger'* ..., and J.-C. Pariente, 'L'Etranger et son double,' *Albert Camus* 1, 'Autour de *L'Etranger*' (1968) 53-80.

13 Cf. Roger Quilliot, 'Un monde ambigu,' *Preuves* 110 (avril 1960) 28-38; Adele King, 'Structure and Meaning in *La Chute*,' *PMLA* LXXVII 5 (Dec. 1962) 660-7; Barbara C. Royce, '*La Chute* and *Saint Genet*: The Question of Guilt,' *The French Review* XXXIX 5 (April 1966) 709-16; Warren Tucker, '*La Chute*, voie du salut terrestre,' *The French Review* XLIII 5 (April 1970) 737-44; and Brian T. Fitch, 'Locuteur, délocuteur et allocutaire dans *La Chute* de Camus' in *L'Analyse du discours/Discourse Analysis*, ed. Pierre R. Léon and Henri Mitterand (Montréal: Centre Educatif et Culturel, Inc. 1976) 123-35.

14 Cf. Brian T. Fitch, 'Le statut précaire du personnage et de l'univers romanesques chez Camus,' *Symposium* XXIV 3, 'Albert Camus II' (Fall 1970) 218-21 and 227-8.

15 Cf. '*L'Etranger*' *d'Albert Camus: un texte ...* 153-5. This stylization is also related to certain structural properties of the novels due to the creation of what I termed an 'inner space' ('Aesthetic Distance and Inner Space in the Novels of Camus,' *Modern Fiction Studies* X 3) 'Albert Camus Special Number' [Autumn 1964] 279-92), a concept later developed in 'L'Espace intérieur' 46-72 in *Narrateur et narration ...*, 2nd ed. (1968).

16 Cf. 'L'Intelligence et l'échafaud.'

17 Cf. Jean-Paul Sartre, 'L'Explication de *L'Etranger*.'

18 Jean Ricardou, *Le Nouveau Roman* (Paris: Seuil 1973) 31

19 Not that the existent criticism on Camus shows any awareness of this essential feature of his fiction

20 Cf. Brian T. Fitch, 'Narcisse interprète: *La Chute* comme modèle herméneutique' (to appear in *Albert Camus* 10, 'Nouvelles Approches').

CHAPTER ONE: THE WRITING ON THE BLACKBOARD

1 Cf. Lucien Dällenbach, *Le Récit spéculaire: essai sur la mise en abyme* (Paris: Seuil 1977) 33n1.

2 Edwin P. Grobe, 'Camus and the Parable of the Perfect Sentence,' *Symposium* XXIV 3, 'Albert Camus II' (Fall 1970) 254

3 Dällenbach gives the following definition of this expression: 'l'on entendra par *mise en abyme de l'énonciation* (1) la 'présentification' diégétique du producteur ou du récepteur du récit, (2) la mise en évidence de la production ou de la réception comme telles, (3) la manifestation du contexte qui conditionne (qui a conditionné) cette production-réception.' (*Le Récit spéculaire* 100). My usage of the term in these pages corresponds to the second of these definitions, although in the case of Grand's sentence, the first category is also involved.

4 The English word *enunciation* does not adequately render the French term *énonciation*, nor does the usual translation *utterance*, since *énoncia-*

tion comprises both the production *and the reception* of the *énoncé*. (Cf. Jean Dubois *et al.*, *Dictionnaire de linguistique* [Paris: Larousse 1973] 192: 'l'énonciation est constituée par l'ensemble des facteurs et des actes qui provoquent la production d'un énoncé. ELLE ENGLOBE LA COMMUNICATION, qui n'en est forcément qu'un cas particulier.') I therefore maintain the French term throughout this book.

5 In *Albert Camus* 6, 'Camus nouvelliste: *L'Exil et le royaume*' (1973) 67-87

6 Linda Hutcheon, '"Le Renégat ou un esprit confus" comme nouveau récit' *Albert Camus* 6, 'Camus nouvelliste: *L'Exil et le Royaume*' (1973) 75

7 Jean Ricardou, *Le Nouveau Roman* (Paris: Seuil 1973) 31

8 José Ortega y Gasset, *The Dehumanization of Art and Other Writings on Art and Culture* (New York: Doubleday Anchor Books 1956) 9-10

9 See my essay, 'Le Statut précaire du personnage et de l'univers romanesques chez Camus,' *Symposium* XXIV 3, 'Albert Camus II' (Fall 1970) 218-29.

10 Ortega y Gasset, *The Dehumanization of Art ...* 10

CHAPTER TWO: THE AUTOREFERENTIAL TEXT: *LA PESTE*

1 It would be tedious and of little utility to the reader to list all 170 page references here.

2 Cf. Peter Cryle, '*La Peste* et le monde concret: étude abstraite,' *Albert Camus* 8, 'Camus romancier: *La Peste*' (1976) 9-25.

3 Jean Ricardou, 'Penser la littérature aujourd'hui,' *Marche romane* XXI, 1-2 (1971) 14

4 *Ibid.*

5 *Ibid.*

6 *Ibid.*

7 Jean Ricardou, *Problèmes du Nouveau Roman* (Paris: Seuil 1967) 11

8 In these pages, I shall use the French term *enchâssement* and the English term *embedding* as synonymous expressions.

9 Tzvetan Todorov, *Poétique de la prose* (Paris: Seuil 1971) 85

10 I owe the formulation of this concept of a '*prenarrator*' with respect to *La Peste* to Janet Paterson in a paper given to my graduate seminar on Camus at the University of Toronto in 1974.

11 Cf. 'Le Statut précaire du personnage et de l'univers romanesques chez Camus,' *Symposium* XXIV 3, 'Albert Camus II' (Fall 1970) 221-2.

12 An analogous phenomenon is to be found at work in the structuring of Georges Bataille's *Le Bleu du ciel* (Paris: Union Générale d'Editions 1957). See my study: '*Le Bleu du ciel' ou le texte réversible* [Toronto:

Department of French, University of Toronto, 'Travaux du Cercle
Méthodologique: monographies, prépublications et documents de
travail' 1980 (to be published as a chapter in *Monde à l'envers/Texte
réversible: la fiction de Bataille* by *Lettres Modernes*)].

13 Sylvère Lotringer, 'Une Révolution romanesque' 327-48 in *Nouveau
Roman: hier, aujourd'hui. 1. Problèmes généraux* (Paris: Union Générale
d'Editions 1972) cf. 336

CHAPTER THREE: THE SELF-GENERATING TEXT: 'JONAS'

1 For an analogous study of the generation of a text through (a) play
on/with words, see my essay: 'A Critique of Roland Barthes' Essay on
Bataille's *Histoire de l'œil*' in *Interpretation of Narrative*, ed. Mario J.
Valdés and Owen J. Miller (Toronto: University of Toronto Press
1978) 48-57, and the second part, entitled 'Textualité,' of my study of
Beckett's trilogy: *Dimensions, structures et textualité dans la trilogie romanesque
de Beckett* (Paris: Lettres Modernes 1977) 127-83.

2 Albert Camus, *Carnets: janvier 1942-mars 1951* (Paris: Gallimard 1964)

3 Cf. Carl A. Viggiani, 'Notes pour le futur biographe d'Albert Camus,'
Albert Camus 1, 'Autour de *L'Etranger*' (1968) 206.

4 Cf. Adele King, 'Jonas ou l'artiste au travail,' *French Studies* XX 3 (July
1966) 270-2.

5 Jean Ricardou, 'Penser la littérature aujourd'hui,' *Marche romane* XXI
1-2 (1971) 14

6 Roland Barthes, *S/Z* (Paris: Seuil 1970) 20-1

7 See Chapter 6 of this book.

8 Ricardou, 'Penser la littérature aujourd'hui' 14

9 Roland Barthes, 'De l'œuvre au texte,' *Revue d'esthétique* 3 (1971) 230

10 *Ibid.* 226-7

CHAPTER FOUR: THE HERMENEUTIQUE PARADIGM: *L'ETRANGER*

1 Lucien Dällenbach, *Le récit spéculaire: essai sur la mise en abyme* (Paris:
Seuil 1977).

2 See '*L'Etranger*' de Camus: un texte, ses lecteurs, leurs lectures* (Paris: Larousse
1972) and particularly its 'Bibliographie critique' (pp 157-73) of 104
items.

3 Cf. Robert Champigny, *Sur un héros païen* (Paris: Gallimard 1959) and
Brian T. Fitch, 'La signification du titre' 93-7 in '*L'Etranger*' de Camus:
un texte ...

4 Cf. 'Le caractère de Meursault' 97-103 in *ibid.*

5 Cf. 'L'Ironie' 103-5 in *ibid.*

6 Cf. 'Le meurtre' 105-9 in *ibid.*

7 M.-G. Barrier, *L'Art du récit dans 'l'Etranger' d'Albert Camus* (Paris: Nizet 1962)

8 J.-C. Pariente, 'L'Etranger et son double,' *Albert Camus* 1, 'Autour de L'Etranger' (1968) 53-80

9 Champigny, *Sur un héros païen*

10 Brian T. Fitch, *Narrateur et narration dans 'L'Etranger' d'Albert Camus* (Paris: Lettres Modernes 1960)

11 Cf. 'La Perspective narrative,' 115-19 in *'L'Etranger' de Camus: un texte ...*

12 Cf. *ibid.* 118-19.

13 René Girard was one of the first critics to develop this parallel in his important article 'Camus' Stranger Retried,' *PMLA* LXXIX 5 (Dec. 1964) 519-33.

14 Cf. *'L'Etranger' de Camus: un texte ...* 113-14.

15 'Camus' Stranger Retried' *PMLA* LXXIX 5 (December 1964) 519

16 *Ibid.* 523

17 As is done by Conor Cruise O'Brien (*Camus*, London: Fontana/Collins 1970) among others. Cf. 'Lecture politique' 32-7 in *'L'Etranger' de Camus: un texte ...*

18 Note, for example, the rôle of the curious form of free indirect reported speech I have analysed elsewhere (cf. 'Aspects de l'emploi du discours indirect libre dans *L'Etranger*,' *Albert Camus* 1, 'Autour de L'Etranger' [1968] 81-91).

19 Jean Onimus, *Camus* (Paris: Desclée de Brouwer 1965) 65-6

20 Pierre-Henri Simon, *Présence de Camus* (Paris: Nizet 1962) 48

21 Charles Moeller, *Littérature du XXe siècle et christianisme. I. Silence de Dieu* (Tournai-Paris: Casterman 1954) 55

22 Pierre Descaves, 'Albert Camus et le roman,' *La Table ronde* 146 (février 1960) 52-3

23 Cf. *Narrateur et narration ...*, 2nd ed. (1968) 27-39.

24 Cf. *'L'Etranger' d'Albert Camus: un texte ...* 99-101.

25 For a detailed analysis of the problems this gives rise to for the reader, see *Narrateur et narration ...*, 2nd ed. (1968) 47-54

26 Philip Thody, 'Meursault et la critique,' *La Revue des Lettres Modernes* VIII 64-6, 'Configuration critique d'Albert Camus' (automne 1961) 15

27 Carina Gadourek, *Les Innocents et les coupables: essai d'exégèse de l'œuvre d'Albert Camus* (La Haye: Mouton 1963) 52

28 *Ibid.* 60

29 The most conclusive support for this account of Camus' strategy in
   L'Etranger is to be found in certain pages of *L'Homme révolté* where he
   discusses the technique of the American novel of the thirties and
   forties which 'prétend trouver son unité en réduisant l'homme soit
   à l'élémentaire, soit à ses réactions extérieures et à son com-
   portement.' (II, 668) The affinities between such a technique and the
   first part of *L'Etranger* are obvious and it is significant that Camus
   attributes to the former the following consequences: 'Ce roman, purgé
   de vie intérieure, où les hommes semblent observés derrière une
   vitre, finit logiquement, en se donnant comme sujet unique, l'homme
   supposé moyen, par mettre en scène le pathologique.' (II, 669)
30 David Madden, 'Camus' *The Stranger*: An Achievement in Simultaneity,' *Renascence* XX (Summer 1968) 189
31 John Cruickshank, *The Novelist as Philosopher: Studies in French Fiction
   1935-60* (London: Oxford University Press 1962) 222
32 Cf. *Narrateur et narration* ..., 2nd ed. (1968) 40-5.
33 Cf. Brian T. Fitch, 'Aspects de l'emploi du discours indirect libre dans
   l'Etranger,' *Albert Camus* 1, 'Autour de *L'Etranger*' (1968).
34 Roger Shattuck was, to my knowledge, the first critic to be struck by
   this passage, commenting on it thus: 'This instant, in which Meursault
   glimpses just a corner of his existence in the mirror, this little still-life
   image of his surroundings, is the first of a series of happenings that
   force Meursault to see himself, to reflect on his life.' ('Two Inside Narratives: *Billy Budd* and *L'Etranger*,' *Texas Studies in Literature and
   Language* IV 3 [Autumn 1962] 317). For a study of the mirror in
   Camus' fiction, see Owen J. Miller, 'L'Image du miroir dans l'œuvre
   romanesque de Camus,' *Albert Camus* 3, 'Sur *La Chute*' (1970) 129-50.
35 For a different commentary on this curious passage, see my 'Lecture
   ontologique,' 71-8 in *'L'Etranger' d'Albert Camus: un texte* ..., cf. 76-7,
   and 'Meursault et les autres' 208-13 in Brian T. Fitch, *Le Sentiment
   d'étrangeté chez Malraux, Sartre, Camus et S. de Beauvoir* (Paris: Lettres
   Modernes 1964).
36 Emile Benveniste, 'De la subjectivité dans le langage' 258-66 in
   Problèmes de linguistique générale, 1 (Paris: Gallimard 1966) cf. 262.
37 *Ibid.* 263
38 *Ibid.* 260
39 Emile Benveniste, 'La Nature des pronoms' 251-7 in *Problèmes de
   linguistic générale*, cf. 254.
40 Georges Poulet, *La Conscience critique* (Paris: Corti 1971) 281
41 Benveniste, 'De la subjectivité dans le langage' 265

42 *Ibid.* 263
43 *Théorie de la littérature: textes des Formalistes russes réunis, présentés et traduits par Tzvetan Todorov* (Paris: Seuil 1965) 51, 217, and 300-1
44 Karin Holter, 'Meursault: personnage camusien à la Robbe-Grillet?,' *Revue romane* VI fasc. 1 (1971) 17

CHAPTER FIVE: THE INTERPRETER INTERPRETED: *LA CHUTE*

1 Wolfgang Iser, *The Implied Reader: Patterns of Communication in Prose Fiction from Bunyan to Beckett* (Baltimore and London: The Johns Hopkins University Press 1974)
2 I shall be returning to the intertextual status of many of these maxims in Chapter 6.
3 Paul Ricoeur, 'What is a Text? Explanation and Interpretation' 135-50 in David M. Rasmussen, *Mythic-Symbolic Language and Philosophical Anthropology: A Constructive Interpretation of the Thought of Paul Ricoeur* (The Hague: Martinus Nijhoff 1971) cf. 145
4 Jean Starobinski, *L'Œil vivant* (Paris: Gallimard 1961) 28
5 Hans-Georg Gadamer, *Truth and Method* (New York: Seabury Press 1975) 238
6 *Ibid.* 274
7 *Ibid.* 289
8 Cf. 'Une Voix qui se parle, qui nous parle, que nous parlons, ou l'espace théâtral de *La Chute*,' *Albert Camus* 3, 'Sur *La Chute*' (1970) 59-79.
9 Gadamer, *Truth and Method* 273
10 *Ibid.*, *loc. cit.*
11 *Ibid.*, *loc. cit.*
12 *Ibid.* 350
13 Wolfgang Iser, *The Act of Reading: A Theory of Aesthetic Response* (Baltimore and London: The Johns Hopkins University Press 1978)
14 Gadamer, *Truth and Method* 317. See also Günther Buck, 'The Structure of Hermeneutic Experience and the Problem of Tradition,' *New Literary History* (Autumn 1978) 31-47, for a detailed analysis of the phenomenon of 'horizonal change due to disappointment of expectation' (p 37).
15 Gadamer, *Truth and Method* 350
16 *Ibid.* 351
17 *Ibid.* 353
18 *Ibid.* 354
19 *Ibid.* 331

20 *Ibid*

21 *Ibid*

22 Paul Ricœur, *Interpretation Theory* (Fort Worth, Texas: Texas Christian University Press 1976) 29

23 *Ibid* 32

24 Ricœur, 'What is a Text? ...' 146

25 Gadamer, *Truth and Method* 354

CHAPTER SIX: JUST BETWEEN TEXTS: INTRA-INTERTEXTUALITY

1 The various types of intertextuality have been identified by Jean Ricardou within what he terms 'l'immense champ de l'intertexte' as follows: 'dans l'intertexte général ou ensemble de tous les textes, se précisent, en soulevant à chaque fois leurs problèmes spécifiques, divers intertextes restreints, ou ensembles des textes entretenant avec le texte en cause une relation construite outre tel rapport intertextuel particulier: les textes du même signataire; les textes de signataires différents et réunis dans un même livre; les textes évoqués dans un texte; les textes dont chacun, sans appartenir à aucune des catégories précédentes, entretient un nombre si élevé de rapports intertextuels avec le texte en cause, qu'il bénéficie d'un effet de présomption dont le principe, en tout occurrence, ne saurait manquer d'être établi' (*Nouveaux Problèmes du roman* [Paris: Seuil 1978] 129).

2 In other words, Ricardou's category of 'les textes du même signataire' (*Nouveaux Problèmes du roman*)

3 Cf. David G. Speer, 'Meursault's Newsclipping,' *Modern Fiction Studies* XIV 2 (Summer 1968) 225-9; Mireille Frauenrath, 'Correspondance,' *Modern Fiction Studies* XVI 1 (Spring 1970) 101-2; and David G. Speer, 'Discussion: More about Meursault's Newsclipping,' *ibid* 102-4.

4 For the sake of completeness, I should mention here the second chapter of *L'Etranger* recounting the Sunday afternoon Meursault spends sitting on his balcony. This is taken in its entirety from Camus' posthumously published work *La Mort heureuse*, where it constitutes a part of the second chapter (cf. *MH* 44-7). However, this latter text cannot be considered to be part of the Camusian canon since its author had no intention of publishing it. While, as a whole, it is substantially different from *L'Etranger*, it does represent the author's first attempt at novel writing and, in a sense, a first version of the later novel. The status of the relationship between the two virtually identical passages is therefore quite different from the intra-intertextual mirroring effect we are studying in this chapter, such as the passage in Tarrou's diary in

La Peste where he notes: 'Question: comment faire pour ne pas perdre son temps? Réponse: passer des journées entières dans l'anti-chambre d'un dentiste, sur une chaise inconfortable; vivre à son balcon le dimanche après-midi ...' (I, 1235). I shall return to this last example a little later.

5 See my article 'Aspects de l'emploi du discours indirect libre dans *L'Etranger*' (*Albert Camus* 1, 'Autour de *L'Etranger* [1968]) for the various effects, ironical and humorous, created by this stylistic trait in Camus' first novel.

6 See 'Lecture psychanalytique' 78-89 in *'L'Etranger' d'Albert Camus: un texte, ses lecteurs, leurs lectures* (Paris: Larousse 1972) 81-3. For an over-all psychoanalytical account of Camus' works, see Alain Costes, *Albert Camus ou la parole manquante* (Paris: Payot 1973), and the more recent, book-length study by Jean Gassin, *L'Univers symbolique d'Albert Camus: essai d'interprétation psychanalytique* (Paris: Lettres Modernes 1980), as well as the latter's two studies: 'Le Sadisme chez Camus,' *Albert Camus* 6, 'Camus nouvelliste: *L'Exil et le royaume*' (1973) 121-44, and 'De Tarrou à Camus: le symbolisme de la guillotine,' *Albert Camus* 8, 'Camus romancier: *La Peste*' (1976) 73-102.

7 For a comparison between these two writers, see L.S. Roudiez, '*L'Etranger, La Chute*, and the Aesthetic Legacy of Gide,' *The French Review* XXXII 4 (February 1959) 300-10, and Henri Hell, 'Gide et Camus,' *La Table ronde* 146 (février 1960) 22-5.

8 Cf. M.-G. Barrier, *L'Art du récit dans 'l'Etranger' d'Albert Camus* (Paris: Nizet 1962) 23n1, and Pierre-Louis Rey, *Camus 'L'Etranger'* (Paris: Hatier 1970) 27.

9 Cf. Linda Hutcheon, '"Le Renégat ou un esprit confus" comme nouveau récit,' *Albert Camus* 6, 'Camus nouvelliste: *L'Exil et le royaume*' (1973)

10 See, for example, René Girard's illuminating study, 'Camus' Stranger Retried'.

11 See, for example, Robert Champigny's *Sur un héros païen*.

12 Cf. 'Lecture politique' 32-7 in *'L'Etranger' d'Albert Camus: un texte ...*, and Conor Cruise O'Brien, *Camus* (London: Fontana/Collins 1970).

13 Cf. Donald Haggis, *Albert Camus: 'La Peste'* (Woodbury, NY: Barron's Educational Series, Inc. 1962)

14 See my study: 'Clamence en chute libre: la cohérence imaginaire de *La Chute*' in *Camus 1970. Colloque organisé sous les auspices du Département des Langues et Littératures Romanes de l'Université de Floride (Gainesville) les 29 et 30 janvier 1970* (Sherbrooke [Canada]: CELEF 1970) 49-68 (cf. p 50), where I attempted a purely formal study of this complex text on the level of the imagery related to its title.

15 For a perceptive and thorough discussion of this particular literary phenomenon, I refer the reader to Valerie Raoul's *The French Fictional Journal: Fictional Narcissism/Narcissistic Fiction* (Toronto: University of Toronto Press 1980).

16 Cf. Owen J. Miller, 'L'Image du miroir dans l'œuvre romanesque de Camus'.

17 Cf. 'La *figuration* peut opérer d'un ouvrage à l'autre du même auteur. C'est ici que cette notion problématique qu'est "l'œuvre d'un écrivain" peut retrouver une pertinence. Les différents textes d'un auteur apparaissent comme autant de variations les uns des autres, ils se commentent, et s'éclairent mutuellement.' (Tzvetan Todorov, *Poétique de la prose* [Paris: Seuil 1971] 250)

Bibliography of Works Cited

BOOKS ON CAMUS

Banks, G.V. *Camus: 'L'Etranger'* (London: Edward Arnold 1976)
Barrier, M.-G. *L'Art du récit dans 'l'Etranger' d'Albert Camus* (Paris: Nizet 1962)
Castex, Pierre-Georges *Albert Camus et 'L'Etranger'* (Paris: Corti 1965)
Champigny, Robert *Sur un héros païen* (Paris: Gallimard 1959)
Costes, Alain *Albert Camus ou la parole manquante* (Paris: Payot 1973)
Cruickshank, John *The Novelist as Philosopher: Studies in French Fiction 1935-60* (London: Oxford University Press 1962)
Cryle, Peter *Bilan critique: 'L'Exil et le royaume' d'Albert Camus: essai d'analyse* (Paris: Lettres Modernes 1973)
Fitch, Brian T. *Narrateur et narration dans 'L'Etranger' d'Albert Camus* (Paris: Lettres Modernes 1960; 2nd revised and enlarged edition 1968)
– *Le Sentiment d'étrangeté chez Malraux, Sartre, Camus et S. de Beauvoir* (Paris: Lettres Modernes 1964)
– *'L'Etranger' d'Albert Camus: un texte, ses lecteurs, leurs lectures* (Paris: Larousse 1972)
Gadourek, Carina, *Les Innocents et les coupables: essai d'exégèse de l'œuvre d'Albert Camus* (La Haye: Mouton 1963)
Gaillard, Pol *Camus: 'La Peste'* (Paris: Hatier 1972)
Gassin, Jean *L'Univers symbolique d'Albert Camus: Essai d'interprétation psychanalytique* (Paris: Lettres Modernes 1980)
Haggis, Donald, *Camus: 'La Peste'* (Woodbury, NY: Barron's Educational Series, Inc. 1962)
Henry, Patrick *Voltaire and Camus: The Limits of Reason and the Awareness of Absurdity* (Banbury, Oxfordshire: The Voltaire Foundation 1975)
Jones, Rosemarie *Camus, 'L'Etranger' and 'La Chute'* (London: Grant and Cutler Ltd 1980)

Maillard, Claudine et Michel *Le Langage en procès: structures et symboles dans 'La Chute' de Camus* (Grenoble: Presses Universitaires de Grenoble 1977)

Moeller, Charles *Littérature du XXe siècle et christianisme. I. Silence de Dieu* (Tournai-Paris: Casterman 1954)

Ngoc Mai, Phan Thi *De la Responsabilité selon 'La Chute' d'Albert Camus* (Saigon: Les Presses de Kim Lai An Quan 1971; limited edition of a thesis presented to the Faculté des Lettres de Saigon)

O'Brien, Conor Cruise *Camus* (London: Fontana/Collins 1970)

Onimus, Jean *Camus* (Paris: Desclée de Brouwer 1965)

Pingaud, Bernard *'L'Etranger' de Camus* (Paris: Hachette 1971)

Rey, Pierre-Louis *Camus: 'L'Etranger'* (Paris: Hatier 1970)

– *Camus: 'La Chute'* (Paris: Hatier 1970)

Albert Camus 1 'Autour de *L'Etranger*' (1968)

Albert Camus 3 'Sur *La Chute*' (1970)

Albert Camus 6 'Camus nouvelliste: *L'Exil et le royaume*' (1973)

Albert Camus 8 'Camus romancier: *La Peste*' (1976)

Albert Camus 10 'Nouvelles Approches' (1981)

OTHER BOOKS

Barthes, Roland *S/Z* (Paris: Seuil 1970)

Benveniste, Emile *Problèmes de linguistique générale, 1* (Paris: Gallimard 1966)

Dällenbach, Lucien *Le Récit spéculaire: essai sur la mise en abyme* (Paris: Seuil 1977)

Dubois, Jean, et al. *Dictionnaire de linguistique* (Paris: Larousse 1973)

Fitch, Brian T. *Dimensions, structures et textualité dans la trilogie romanesque de Beckett* (Paris: Lettres Modernes 1977)

– *Monde à l'envers/Texte réversible: la fiction de Bataille* (to be published by Lettres Modernes)

– *'Le Bleu du ciel' ou le texte réversible* (Toronto: Department of French, University of Toronto, 'Travaux du Cercle Méthodologique: monographies, prépublications et documents de travail' 1980)

Gadamer, Hans-Georg *Truth and Method* (New York: Seabury Press 1975) (translated from the German: *Wahrheit und Methode* [Tübingen: J.C.B. Mohr 1960])

Hutcheon, Linda *Narcissistic Narrative: The Metafictional Paradox* (Waterloo: Wilfrid Laurier University Press 1980)

Iser, Wolfgang *The Implied Reader: Patterns of Communication in Prose Fiction from Bunyan to Beckett* (Baltimore and London: The Johns Hopkins Uni-

versity Press 1974) (translated from the German: *Der Implizite Leser: Kommunikationsformen des Romans von Bunyan bis Beckett* [Munich: Wilhelm Fink 1972])
– *The Act of Reading: A Theory of Aesthetic Response* (Baltimore and London: The Johns Hopkins University Press 1978) (translated from the German: *Der Akt des Lesens. Theorie ästhetischer Wirkung* [Munich: Wilhelm Fink 1976])
Ortega y Gasset, José *The Dehumanization of Art and Other Writings on Art and Culture* (New York: Doubleday Anchor Books 1956)
Poulet, Georges *La Conscience critique* (Paris: Corti 1971)
Raoul, Valerie *The French Fictional Journal: Fictional Narcissism/Narcissistic Fiction* (Toronto: University of Toronto Press 1980)
Ricardou, Jean *Problèmes du Nouveau Roman* (Paris: Seuil 1967)
– *Le Nouveau Roman* (Paris: Seuil 1973)
– *Nouveaux Problèmes du roman* (Paris: Seuil 1978)
Ricœur, Paul 'What is a Text? Explanation and Interpretation' 135-50 in David M. Rasmussen, *Mythic-Symbolic Language and Philosophical Anthropology: A Constructive Interpretation of the Thought of Paul Ricœur* (The Hague: Martinus Nijhoff 1971)
– *Interpretation Theory* (Fort Worth, Texas: Texas Christian University Press 1976)
Starobinski, Jean *L'Œil vivant* (Paris: Gallimard 1961)
Todorov, Tzvetan *Poétique de la prose* (Paris: Seuil 1971)
– *Théorie des la littérature: textes des Formalistes russes réunis, présentés et traduits par Tzvetan Todorov* (Paris: Seuil 1965)

ARTICLES

Abbou, André, '*La Chute* et ses lecteurs: I. Jusqu'en 1962' *Albert Camus* 3, 'Sur *La Chute*' (1970) 9-19
Barthes, Roland 'De l'œuvre au texte' *Revue d'esthétique* 3 (1971) 225-32
Buck, Günther 'The Structure of Hermeneutic Experience and the Problem of Tradition' *New Literary History* (Autumn 1978) 31-47
Camus, Albert 'Lettres au Directeur des *Temps Modernes*' *Les Temps modernes* 82 (août 1952) 317-33
Cryle, Peter '*La Peste* et le monde concret: étude abstraite' *Albert Camus* 8, 'Camus romancier: *La Peste*' (1976) 9-25
Descaves, Pierre 'Albert Camus et le roman' *La Table ronde* 146 (février 1960) 47-60
Fitch, Brian T. 'Aesthetic Distance and Inner Space in the Novels of Camus' *Modern Fiction Studies* x 3 (Autumn 1964) 279-92

- 'Aspects de l'emploi du discours indirect libre dans *L'Etranger*' *Albert Camus* 1, 'Autour de *L'Etranger*' (1968) 81-91
- 'Clamence en chute libre: la cohérence imaginaire de *La Chute*' in *Camus 1970: Colloque organisé sous les auspices du Département des Langues et Littératures Romanes de l'Université de Floride (Gainesville) les 29 et 30 janvier 1970* ed. Raymond Gay-Crosier (Sherbrooke [Canada]: CELEF 1970) 49-68
- 'Le Statut précaire du personnage et de l'univers romanesques chez Camus' *Symposium* XXIV 3, 'Albert Camus II' (Fall 1970) 218-28
- 'Une voix qui se parle, qui nous parle, que nous parlons, ou l'espace théâtral de *La Chute*' *Albert Camus* 3, 'Sur *La Chute*' (1970) 59-79
- '*La Chute* et ses lecteurs: II. Depuis 1962' *ibid.* 20-32
- 'Locuteur, délocuteur et allocutaire dans *La Chute* de Camus' in *L'Analyse du discours/Discourse Analysis*, ed. Pierre R. Léon and Henri Mitterand (Montréal: Centre Educatif et Culturel, Inc. 1976) 123-35
- 'A Critique of Roland Barthes' Essay on Bataille's *Histoire de l'œil*' in *Interpretation of Narrative*, ed. Mario J. Valdes and Owen J. Miller (Toronto: University of Toronto Press 1978) 48-57
- 'Narcisse interprète: *La Chute* comme modèle herméneutique' (to appear in *Albert Camus* 10, 'Nouvelles Approches')
Frauenrath, Mireille 'Correspondance' *Modern Fiction Studies* XVI 1 (Spring 1970) 101-2
Gassin, Jean 'Le Sadisme chez Camus' *Albert Camus* 6, 'Camus nouvelliste: L'Exil et le royaume' (1973) 121-44
- 'De Tarrou à Camus: le symbolisme de la guillotine' *Albert Camus* 8, 'Camus romancier: *La Peste*' (1976) 73-102
Girard, René 'Camus' Stranger Retried' *PMLA* LXXIX 5 (December 1964) 519-33
Grobe, Edwin P. 'Camus and the Parable of the Perfect Sentence' *Symposium* XXIV 3, 'Albert Camus II' (Fall 1970) 254-61
Holter, Karin 'Meursault: personnage camusien à la Robbe-Grillet?' *Revue romane* VI fasc. 1 (1971) 17-24
Hell, Henri 'Gide et Camus' *La Table ronde* 146 (février 1960) 22-5
Hutcheon, Linda '"Le Renégat ou un esprit confus" comme nouveau récit' *Albert Camus* 6, 'Camus nouvelliste: L'Exil et le royaume' (1973) 67-87
Jeanson, Francis 'Pour tout vous dire' *Les Temps modernes* 82 (août 1952) 354-83
King, Adele 'Structure and Meaning in *La Chute*' *PMLA* LXXVII 5 (December 1962) 660-7
- 'Jonas ou l'artiste au travail' *French Studies* XX 3 (July 1966) 267-80

Lotringer, Sylvère, 'Une révolution romanesque' 327-48 in *Nouveau Roman: hier, aujourd'hui. 1. Problèmes généraux* (Paris: Union Générale d'Editions 1972) 327-48

Madden, David 'Camus' *The Stranger*: An Achievement in Simultaneity' *Renascence* XX (Summer 1968) 186-97

Mason, Haydn T. 'Voltaire and Camus' *The Romanic Review* LIX 3 (October 1968) 198-212

Miller, Owen J. 'L'Image du miroir dans l'œuvre romanesque de Camus' *Albert Camus* 3, 'Sur *La Chute*' (1970) 129-50

Pariente, Jean-Claude 'L'Etranger et son double' *Albert Camus* 1, 'Autour de *L'Etranger*' (1968) 53-80

Quilliot, Roger 'Un monde ambigu' *Preuves* 110 (avril 1960) 28-38

Ricardou, Jean, 'Penser la littérature aujourd'hui' *Marche romane* XXI, 1-2 (1971) 7-17

Roudiez, L.S. '*L'Etranger, La Chute* and the Aesthetic Legacy of Gide' *The French Review* XXXII 4 (February 1959) 300-10

Royce, Barbara C. '*La Chute* and *Saint Genet: The Question of Guilt*' *The French Review* XXXIX 5 (April 1966) 709-16

Sartre, Jean-Paul 'Explication de *L'Etranger*' *Cahiers du sud* 253 (1943) 189-206 (reprinted in *Situations I* [Paris: Gallimard 1947] 99-121)

– 'Réponse à Albert Camus' *Les Temps modernes* 82 (août 1952) 334-53

Shattuck, Roger 'Two Inside Narratives: *Billy Budd* and *L'Etranger*' *Texas Studies in Literature and Language* IV 3 (Autumn 1962) 314-20

Speer, David G. 'Meursault's Newsclipping' *Modern Fiction Studies* XIV 2 (Summer 1968) 225-9

– 'Discussion: More about Meursault's Newsclipping' *Modern Fiction Studies* XVI 1 (Spring 1970) 102-4

Thody, Philip 'Meursault et la critique' *La Revue des Lettres Modernes* VIII 64-6, 'Configuration critique d'Albert Camus. I. *L'Etranger* à l'étranger: Camus devant la critique anglo-saxonne,' ed. J.H. Matthews (automne 1961) 11-23

Tucker, Warren '*La Chute*, voie du salut terrestre' *The French Review* XLIII 5 (April 1970) 737-44

Viggiani, Carl A. 'Notes pour le futur biographe d'Albert Camus' *Albert Camus* 1, 'Autour de *L'Etranger*' (1968) 200-18

Author Index

UNIVERSITY OF TORONTO ROMANCE SERIES

This book

was designed by

ANTJE LINGNER

of University of

Toronto

Press